alfred's max™

Learn to play Keyboard

Complete

see it ◉ hear it ◉ play it

D1568611

AMY ROSSER
NATHANIEL GUNOD
KATE WESTIN

Alfred's MAX™ is the next best thing to having your own private teacher. No confusion, no frustration, no guesswork—just lessons that are well paced and easy to follow. You listen to the music you're learning to play and watch a professional show how it's done, then get time to stretch out and put it all together. No matter how you like to learn, Alfred's MAX™ series gives you the ultimate learning experience at a screamin' deal of a price.

Cover foreground keyboard photo by Karen Miller.
Cover background keyboard photo courtesy of Yamaha Corporation of America.

Alfred

Book and DVD (with case)
ISBN-10: 0-7390-4171-1
ISBN-13: 978-0-7390-4171-0

Book and DVD (without case)
ISBN-10: 0-7390-4209-2
ISBN-13: 978-0-7390-4209-0

CONTENTS

Level 1

How to Use This Book and DVD 4

Sitting at Your Instrument 5
  Sitting at the Piano
  Sitting at the Electronic Keyboard

Hand and Finger Position 6
  Fingering

The Keyboard and Pitch 7

Finger Warm-ups on the Black Keys 8

The Musical Alphabet and the
Names of the White Keys 9

Finger Warm-ups on the White Keys 10

Rhythm 11
  Merrily We Roll Along
  Go Tell Aunt Rhody
  Aura Lee

Time Signatures 14
  Right in Time
  Four Beats Left to Go
  Time for Both
  Au Claire de la Lune

The Treble Staff 16
  Old Woman on the Right
  Mary Had a Little Lamb

The Bass Staff 18
  Old Woman on the Left
  Frère Jacques

The Grand Staff 20

The Whole Rest 21
  Ode to Joy
  Frère Jacques—Right and Left
  Ode to Joy (with Two Hands)
  Merrily We Roll Along

The Half Rest 23
  Lightly Row

The Quarter Rest 24
  Quarter March
  A Restful Day
  A Stitch in Time
  Anna's March

Dynamic Markings 26
  Loud and Soft
  Three Ways to Play

Melodic 2nds 28
  Who's on Second?

Melodic 3rds 29
  Third Dimension

Harmonic 2nds and 3rds 30
  Sweet and Sour

Melodic 4ths 31
  Go Fourth and Make Music!

Melodic 5ths 32
  Fifth Avenue

Harmonic 4ths and 5ths 33
  Jingle Bells

Middle C Position 34
  Middle C Rock

The Flat Sign 36
  B Flat, B Blue
  Walk in the Park
  Rockin' All Night Long

G Position 38

Harmonic 3rds, 4ths and 5ths 39
  G Rock

Tied Notes 40
  Tie Exercise

Dotted Half Notes 41
  Auld Lang Syne

$\frac{3}{4}$ Time Signature 42
  Anna's Waltz

The Natural Sign 43
  Tied and True Blues

The C Major Chord 44
  Largo (Theme from the
   New World Symphony)

The Pickup 45
  When the Saints Go Marching In

The G⁷ Chord 46
  Mary Ann

The F Major Chord 48
  For He's a Jolly Good Fellow

Level 2

Eighth Notes & Eighth Rests 50
  Simple Gifts

The Sharp Sign 52
  Für Elise

The Dotted Quarter Note 53
  Eine Kleine Nachtmusik

More Dynamic Markings 55
  Blue and True
  Theme from a Mozart Sonata

Melodic & Harmonic 6ths 57
  Sixth Sense

Melodic & Harmonic 7ths 58
  Seventh Heaven

Octaves 59
  Octaboogie

Half Steps & Whole Steps 60

The Key of C Major 61
  C Major Scale Split

Practicing the C Major Scale 62

Tempo Markings 63
  C Major Scale Exercise

Articulation 64
  Slide, Bounce, and Bang

Ritardandos & Fermatas 65
  Good Morning to You

$\frac{2}{4}$ Time Signature 66
  Russian Folk Dance

Primary Chords 67
  Primary Chords in the Key of C Major
  Primary Progression

Chord Inversions 68
  Solid State

The Sustain Pedal (Damper Pedal) 69
  Bach Prelude in C

The Key of G Major 71
  G Major Scale
  Primary Chords in the Key of G Major

The Key Signature 72
  All Through the Night
  Minuet in G

A Piece in Two Keys .74
  Burleske

Alouette 75

Tempo & Expression 76

Triplets 77
  Beautiful Dreamer

$\frac{6}{8}$ Time Signature 78
  Alphabeats
  The Irish Washerwoman

The Key of F Major 80
  F Major Scale
  Primary Chords in the Key of F Major
  Joy to the World

A Piece in Three Keys 82
  Three-Key Rock

Repeats 83

Minor Keys 84
  Scherzo

Harmonic Minor 86
  Primary Chords in Minor Keys

Symphony No. 40 88

Waves of the Danube 90

The Entertainer 92

Chord Reference 94

Major Scales 112

Minor Scales 117

The Circle of Fifths 132

About the DVD

The DVD contains valuable demonstrations of all the instructional material in the book. You will get the best results by following along with your book as you watch these video segments. Musical examples that are not performed with video are included as audio tracks on the DVD for listening and playing along.

HOW TO USE THIS BOOK AND DVD

Alfred's MAX™ Keyboard Complete provides all the information you need to get started playing any keyboard instrument. The book and DVD may be used together or separately. The DVD contains video demonstrations of the pieces and exercises in the book plus further explanations of techniques and musical concepts to further help you reach your maximum potential on the keyboard.

Like most students, you may find it best to have your DVD player positioned near your instrument so that you can use the book as you watch and play along with the video. Sometimes you might prefer to work first with the book before using the video, carefully reading the instructions and playing the music. Other times, you may want to start by watching the demonstration. You decide what works best for you. There is no wrong way to use an Alfred's MAX book and DVD!

If you have an acoustic piano, whether it is a spinet, upright, or grand piano, you have all of the advantages of wonderful *touch sensitivity*. This means that you will be in complete control of the type of piano sound you make.

If you are just getting started and do not own a piano, it is a good idea to buy an electronic keyboard that is completely portable. Many keyboards will even operate with batteries and have their own internal speakers. Perhaps the most interesting feature of an electronic keyboard is the opportunity to choose different sounds for each piece of music. You will find suggestions in this method for different sounds to use. When shopping for an electronic keyboard, it is a good idea to choose one that has touch-sensitive keys so that you can vary the loudness and softness of the music with the force of your touch.

Here are some important things anyone learning to play music should keep in mind:

- **It is better to practice a little a lot than to practice a lot a little**. In other words, never miss a day of practice, even if you spend just a few minutes. Skipping a few days of practice and then practicing once for a long time will not be nearly as helpful as regular practice.

- **The quickest way to play fast fluently is to take the slowest route.** You will learn to play fast music by practicing slowly. Playing too fast too soon can lead to confusion, difficulty and bad habits that will slow your progress. The tortoise wins the race!

- **Practice with a metronome.** A metronome is an adjustable device that beats time for you. Electronic metronomes are inexpensive and very accurate. Get one that makes a click loud enough for you to hear. Practicing with a metronome will teach you to play with correct rhythm.

Although this book is perfect for a self-directed student, **there is no substitute for a good teacher.** A teacher can watch and listen to you play, and give you guidance and encouragement to do your best.

SITTING AT YOUR INSTRUMENT

Sitting at the Piano

- The bench must face the keyboard squarely.

- Sit on the edge of the bench exactly in front of the middle of the keyboard.

- Lean slightly forward.

- Relax and let your arms hang loosely from the shoulders.

- Adjust the distance of the bench from the keyboard so that when your hands are on the keyboard, your arms are parallel to the floor.

- Your knees should be slightly under the keyboard.

- Your feet should be flat on the floor. One foot may be slightly forward.

Sitting at the Electronic Keyboard

This is exactly the same as sitting at the piano, but be careful with the height of the stand or table on which the keyboard is sitting. Adjust the keyboard stand or the table/chair combination you are using so that your arms are perpendicular to and level with the keyboard.

HAND AND FINGER POSITION

- Curve your fingers. From above, you should see a row of knuckles but no fingernails.

- Curve the thumb slightly inward. No hitchhiker thumbs!

- There should be a hollow spot big enough for a ping-pong ball to fit in your palm.

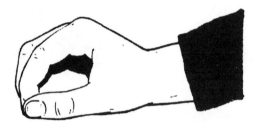

- Fingers are used like levers with the motion coming from the joint that attaches the finger to the hand.

- Push the keys down with the tips of the fingers.

- Keep your fingernails very short!

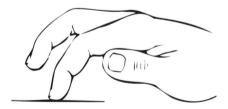

Fingering

Fingering numbers, which appear as the numbers 1 through 5, show which fingers to use to play. They can be found above or below the music. Each number corresponds to the same finger on either hand, with both thumbs being number 1 and both pinkies being number 5.

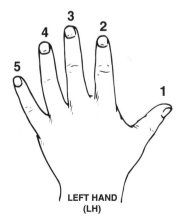 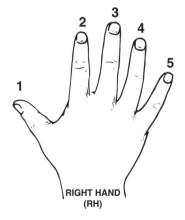

LEFT HAND (LH)   RIGHT HAND (RH)

THE KEYBOARD AND PITCH

The *keyboard* is made up of white and black *keys.* These keys are laid out in a repeating pattern, with black keys in groups of two and three. Each group of black keys is separated by two white keys.

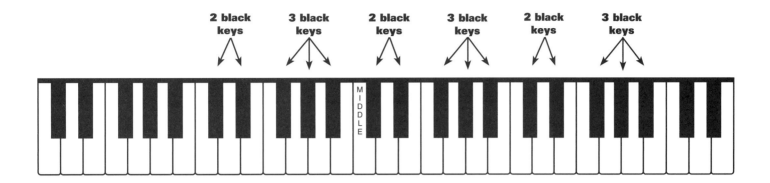

Pitch is the highness or lowness of a sound. On the piano keyboard, the pitch goes down to the left, and goes up to the right. As you move to the left, the pitches sound lower. As you move to the right, the pitches sound higher.

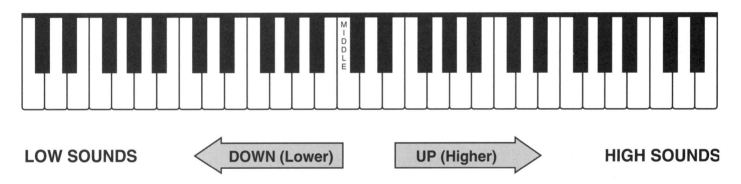

LOW SOUNDS   ⬅ DOWN (Lower)   UP (Higher) ➡   **HIGH SOUNDS**

Award-winning pianist and singer/songwriter Norah Jones brought new attention to jazz keyboard sounds with her 2002 album *Come Away With Me.* Her unique blend of pop and jazz has made her one of the world's most popular performers.

Photo: © Tim Mosenfelder/Corbis

FINGER WARM-UPS ON THE BLACK KEYS

To get your fingers moving on the keyboard, play these exercises on the black keys.
The illustrations show which fingers to use on which black keys.

The numbers represent the fingers you will use to play.
Read from left to right and play at a slow, even pace.

Black-Key Warm-up for the Right Hand

RH

1	2	3	2	1	1	1
1	2	3	2	3	4	4
5	4	3	2	1	1	1
1	2	3	4	5	1	1

Right Hand (RH)

Black-Key Warm-up for the Left Hand

LH

5	4	3	4	5	5	5
5	4	3	4	3	2	2
1	2	3	4	5	5	5
5	4	3	2	1	5	5

Left Hand (LH)

THE MUSICAL ALPHABET
AND THE NAMES OF THE WHITE KEYS

There are seven letters in the *musical alphabet:*

A B C D E F G

They repeat over and over:

A B C D E F G A B C D E F G A B C and so on.

Every key on the piano has a name from the musical alphabet. The illustration below shows the names of the white keys. Notice that the C nearest the middle of the keyboard is called *middle C.* This is an important marker to memorize.

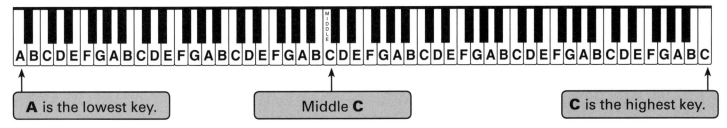

A is the lowest key.   Middle **C**   **C** is the highest key.

If you are using an electronic keyboard with fewer than 88 keys, middle C is still the C closest to the middle of the keyboard. The highest and lowest notes, however, may be different than those shown above.

Notice that every C is always directly to the left of a group of two black keys.

Every F is directly to the left of a group of three black keys.

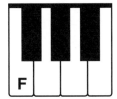

Find all of the C's and all of the F's on your keyboard.

FINGER WARM-UPS ON THE WHITE KEYS

Now let's try playing on the white keys. In these warm-ups, the notes are black circles with the name of the key to be played inside. The finger numbers appear **above** notes played with the right hand (**RH**) and **below** notes played with the left hand (**LH**).

Finger: 1

Note: C

One of the reasons that music notation is easy to read is that it looks the way it sounds. As the pitch goes up, the notes look higher on the page; as the pitch goes down, the notes look lower on the page. The warm-ups below are great examples of this.

Right-Hand Warm-up No. 1

Start on middle C. This is the right-hand C Position.

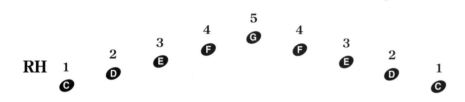

Right-Hand Warm-up No. 2

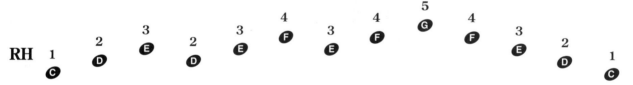

Left-Hand Warm-up No. 1

Start on the C below middle C. This is the left-hand C Position.

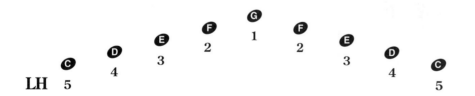

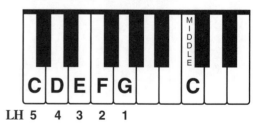

Left-Hand Warm-up No. 2

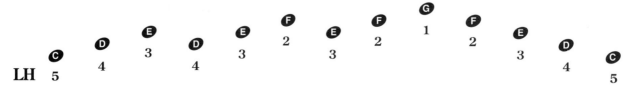

RHYTHM

Rhythm is the arrangement of long and short sounds into patterns. We measure the lengths of these sounds by counting *beats*. A beat is a unit of musical time; it is the pulse that keeps the music alive. When you tap your foot as you listen to music, you are tapping the beats.

We write rhythms with notes.

Play four quarter notes on middle C with your right hand. Count four steady beats aloud ("1, 2, 3, 4"), giving each quarter note one beat.

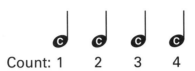

Count: 1   2   3   4

Play two half notes on middle C with your right hand.
Count four steady beats aloud, giving each half note two beats.

Count: 1   2   3   4

Play a whole note on middle C with your right hand.
Count four steady beats aloud.

Count: 1   2   3   4

Using the music below as a guide, first play four quarter notes on middle C with your right hand, one note for each count. Then, play two half notes, playing one note for every two counts. Then play a whole note, counting to four while you hold the note. Each group of four counts, or beats, is called a *measure*. Music is divided into measures with *bar lines*, and a *double bar* is used at the end.

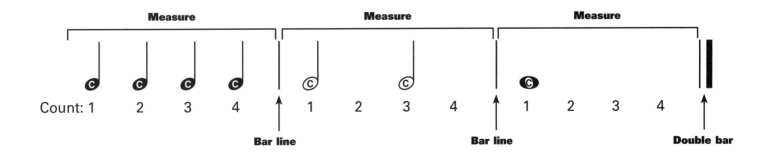

Enjoy playing these melodies. At first, count aloud as you play.

After you learn to play these, experiment with your electronic keyboard and try playing them with some interesting sounds.

Merrily We Roll Along

Traditional

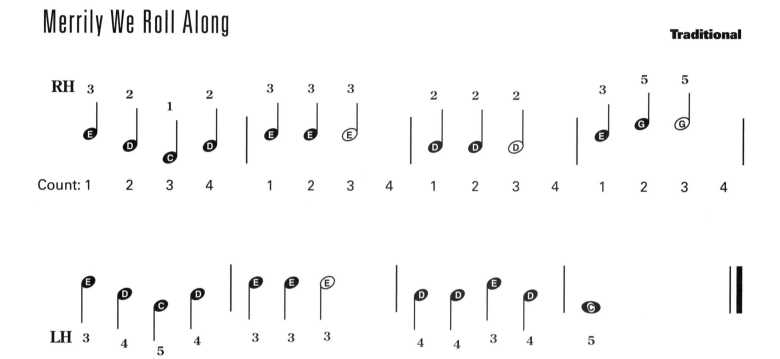

Billy Joel discovered classical piano music at the age of four, and his love for the style that provided such a great technical foundation for his playing has never ended. With a smart urban sensibility and tremendous talent for composing music in a variety of styles, he is considered to be one of the most influential singer/songwriters of our time.

Photo: © Ken Settle

Go Tell Aunt Rhody

Traditional

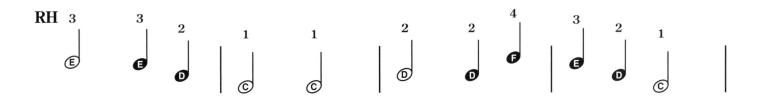

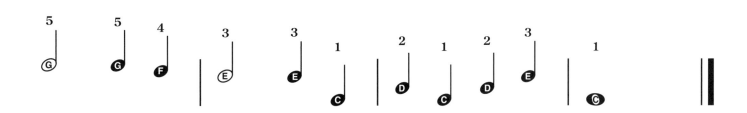

Aura Lee

Traditional

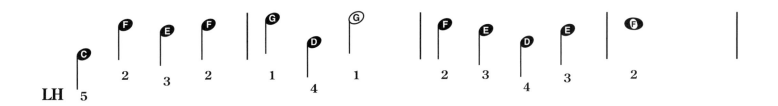

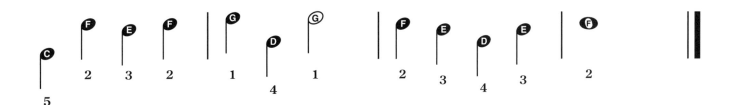

TIME SIGNATURES

At the beginning of every piece of music are numbers called the *time signature.* The time signature tells us how to count the music.

4 The top number tells how many beats are in each measure.
A **4** means there are **four** beats in each measure.

4 The bottom number tells what kind of note gets one beat.
A **4** means a **quarter note** ♩ gets one beat.

Right in Time

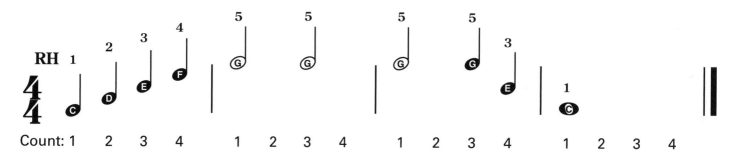

Four Beats Left to Go

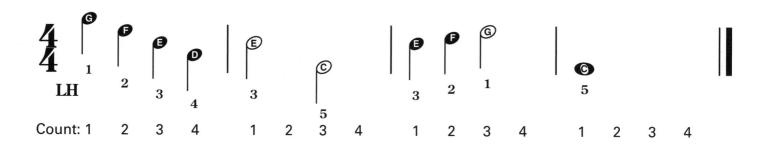

Count carefully and keep a steady beat.

Try a flute sound for these pretty tunes!

Time for Both

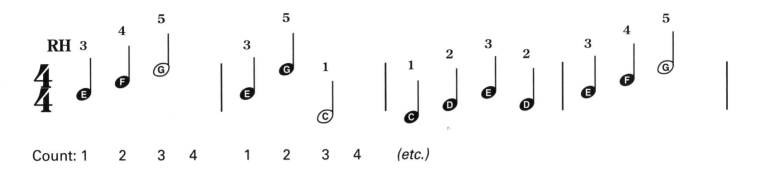

Count: 1 2 3 4 1 2 3 4 (etc.)

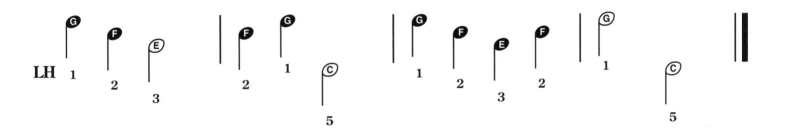

Au Clair de la Lune

French Folk Song

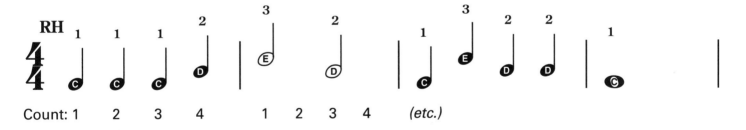

Count: 1 2 3 4 1 2 3 4 (etc.)

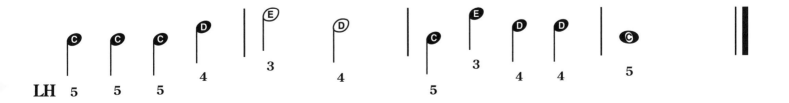

THE TREBLE STAFF

In music notation, specific notes are indicated by their placement on a *staff*, which is made of five horizontal lines and the four spaces in between.

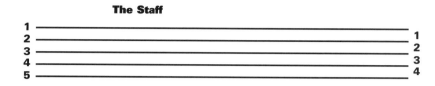

The Staff

Music for the right hand is written on the *treble staff*, which is marked with a *treble clef*. The treble clef is sometimes called the *G clef* because the line it encircles is called G. A note placed on that line will be a G note.

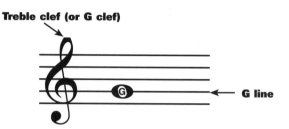

Treble clef (or G clef)

←— G line

As the music moves up through the musical alphabet, each note is written on the next-higher space or line. As the music moves down—backward through the alphabet—each note is written on the next-lower space or line. Notice that D is written on the space just below the staff, and middle C is written on a short line below the staff called a *leger line*.

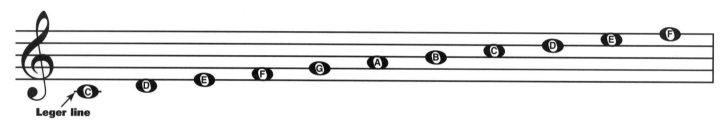

Leger line

The spaces of the treble staff are easy to remember because, from bottom to top, they spell the word **FACE**.

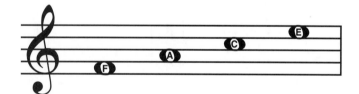

You can remember the notes on the lines of the treble staff using the sentence **E**very **G**ood **B**oy **D**oes **F**ine.

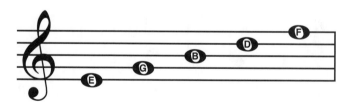

Here is the right-hand C position and the notes on the treble staff.

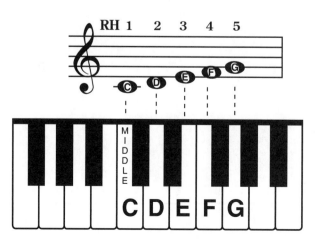

Here are some C-position pieces on the treble staff for you to play. As you can see, the music still looks the way it sounds: As the pitch ascends, the notes look higher on the page; as the pitch descends, the notes look lower on the page. Longer notes take more space, shorter notes take less space.

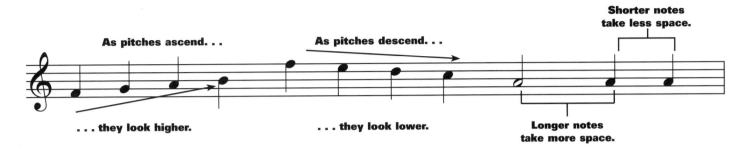

Old Woman on the Right

Traditional

Mary Had a Little Lamb

Traditional

THE BASS STAFF

Music for the left hand is written on the *bass staff,* which is marked with a *bass clef.* The bass clef is sometimes called the *F clef* because the line surrounded by the dots is called F. A note placed on that line will be an F note.

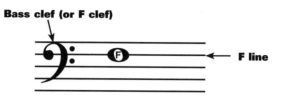

Just like the notes on the treble staff, as the music moves up through the musical alphabet, each note is written on the next-higher space or line. As the music moves down, each note is written on the next-lower space or line.

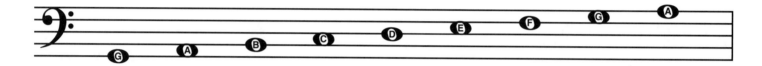

You can remember the notes on the spaces of the bass staff using the sentence **A**ll **C**ows **E**at **G**rass.

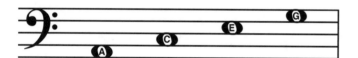

You can remember the notes on the lines of the bass staff using the sentence **G**reat **B**ig **D**ogs **F**ight **A**nimals.

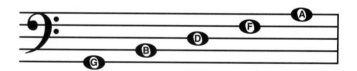

Here is the left-hand C position and the notes on the bass staff.

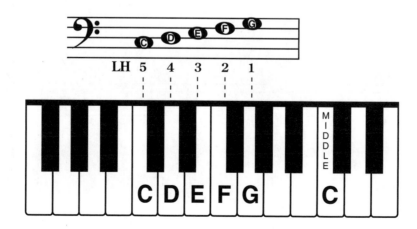

Here are some C-position pieces on the bass staff for you to play.

Old Woman on the Left

Traditional

Frère Jacques

French Folk Song

During a time when the guitar dominated the world of music, Elton John redefined the role of the piano in rock. With a flamboyant style of performing, he became one of the most influential keyboard artists of the 1970s and 1980s. In addition to a phenomenal recording career, he has achieved great success as a composer for hit Broadway musicals such as *Aida* and the *Lion King*.

THE GRAND STAFF

Piano music is written on a *grand staff,* which has a treble staff
and a bass staff that are connected by barlines and a *brace.*

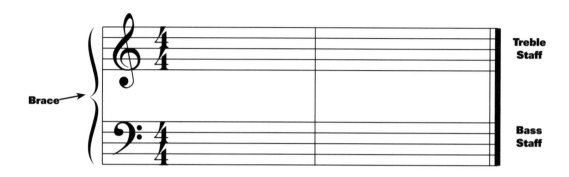

Here is C position and the notes on the grand staff.

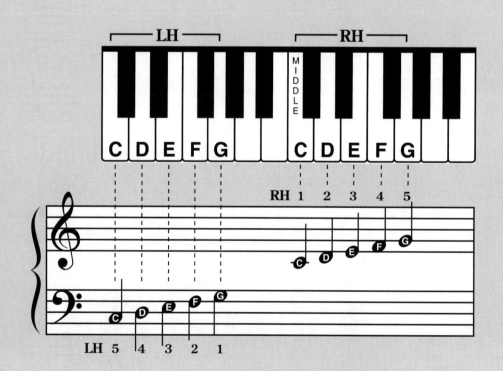

THE WHOLE REST

A *whole rest* indicates an entire measure of silence.

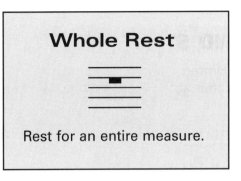

The following pieces will give you some practice reading music on the grand staff. Notice that while one hand is playing, the other is resting.

Try a big orchestral sound for this melody from Beethoven's Ninth Symphony.

Ode to Joy

Ludwig van Beethoven

Frère Jacques—Right and Left

French Folk Song

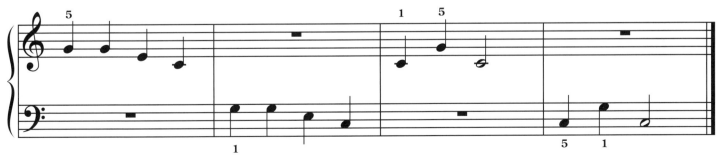

Below is another version of "Ode to Joy." This time, you'll play with both hands together. Keep your hands in C position and keep your eyes on the music. Learning to play by "feel" will make you a better sight-reader.

Practice Tip: It is helpful to learn each hand individually before playing with both together.

Ode to Joy (with Two Hands)

Ludwig van Beethoven

Merrily We Roll Along

Traditional

THE HALF REST

A *half rest* indicates two beats of silence.

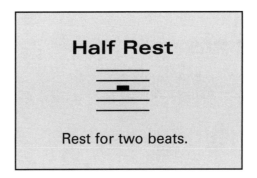

Be careful not to confuse the half rest with the whole rest. Notice that the half rest sits on top of the third line while the whole rest hangs below the fourth line.

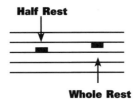

This exercise will prepare you for "Lightly Row," which combines half rests in one hand with notes in the other.

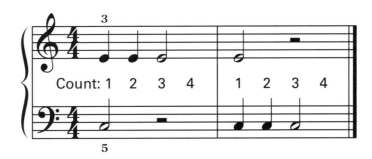

Lightly Row

Traditional

THE QUARTER REST

A *quarter rest* indicates one beat of silence. It looks a little bit like a bird flying sideways.

Quarter Rest

Rest for one beat.

The following pieces will let you concentrate on counting rests because they use only one hand at a time.

Quarter March

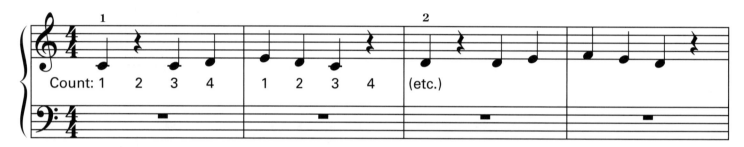

Count: 1   2   3   4   1   2   3   4   (etc.)

A Restful Day

Count: 1   2   3   4   1   2   3   4   1   2   3   4   1   2   3   4

(etc.)

Let's put the hands back together. First, learn each hand individually, counting carefully. Remember to keep your eyes on the music.

A Stitch in Time

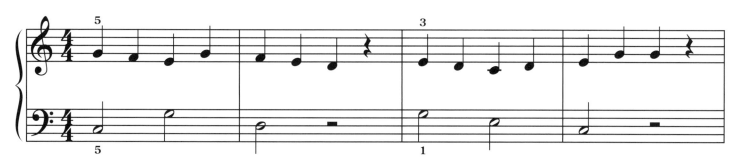

Anna's March

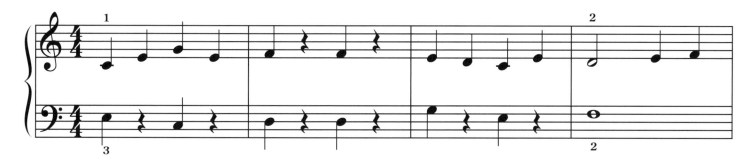

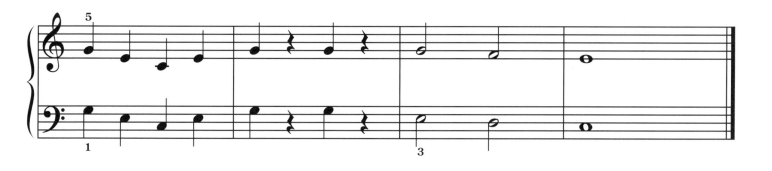

DYNAMIC MARKINGS

One of the ways we make music more enjoyable and interesting is by varying the volume at which we play. Musicians refer to these changes in volume as *dynamics*, and *dynamic markings* are used in written music to indicate the various degrees of loud and soft.

Below are two important dynamic markings. Each one is an abbreviation of an Italian word that describes the volume. (Italian is the international language of music.)

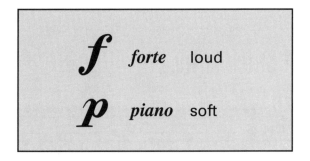

On a keyboard with weighted keys (such as an acoustic piano and some electronic keyboards), play loud by using more weight in the arm and wrist as you drop into the key; use less weight to play soft. On a keyboard that does not have weighted keys, use a more forceful finger motion to play loud, and use a more gentle finger motion to play soft.

Electronic Keyboards: If you are playing an electronic keyboard with touch-sensitive keys, you will be able to affect dynamics with your fingers as described above. If your keyboard does not have touch-sensitive keys, you may have to change the sound selection or use the volume control to create changes in dynamics.

Play all the loud notes equally loud and all the soft notes equally soft. Keep a steady beat, and be careful not to play faster when you play louder or slower when you play softer. Have fun with this study in contrasts.

Loud and Soft

Here is another important dynamic marking:

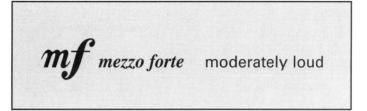

Concentrate on making a clear difference between the different dynamics in this piece.

Three Ways to Play

Tori Amos began playing piano at the young age of two and a half. With her original, technically fluid keyboard stylings and remarkable talent for elegant, inventive songwriting, she began attracting what is now a huge loyal following with the release of her 1992 album *Little Earthquakes*.

Photo: © Ken Settle

MELODIC 2NDS

An *interval* is the distance between two notes. On the keyboard, the interval from one white key to another adjacent white key, up or down, is called a *2nd*. When two notes are played one after the other, as notes are played in a melody, the interval is called a *melodic interval*.

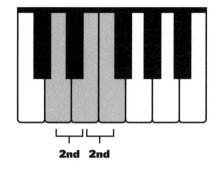

Notice that 2nds are written from a **line to a space**, or a **space to a line**.

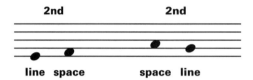

Some of the melodic 2nds in the following piece are labeled for you; see if you can label the rest.

Who's on Second?

MELODIC 3RDS

To play a 3rd, skip a white key.

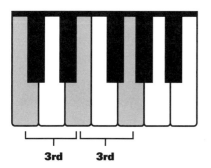

3rd   **3rd**

Notice that 3rds are written from a **line to a line**, or a **space to a space**.

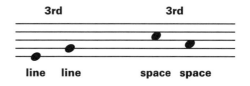

3rd   3rd

line   line   space   space

Some of the melodic 3rds in the next piece are labeled. Try labeling the rest yourself.

Third Dimension

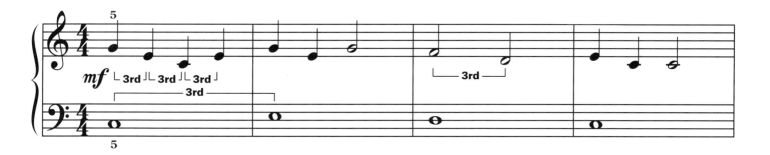

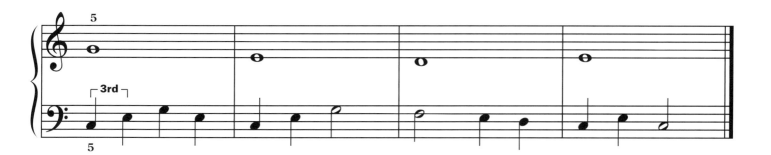

HARMONIC 2NDS & 3RDS

When we play two notes together, we create *harmony*, and the intervals between these notes are called *harmonic intervals*. The 2nds and 3rds you have learned as melodic intervals can also be played as harmonic intervals.

Play these harmonic 2nds and 3rds, and notice that the 2nds have a *dissonant* (clashing) sound and the 3rds have a *consonant* (harmonious, sweet) sound.

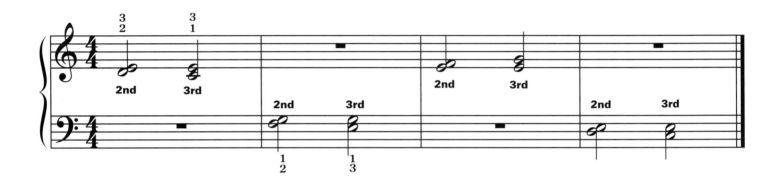

Now that you're playing notes together with a single hand, it is even more important to learn each hand separately before putting them together.

Sweet and Sour

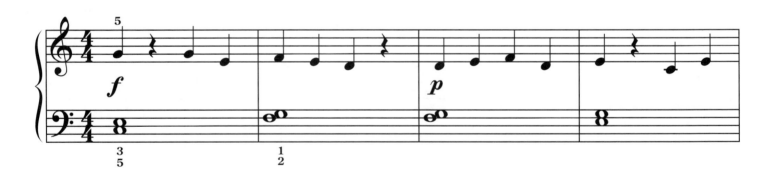

MELODIC 4THS

To play a 4th, skip two white keys.

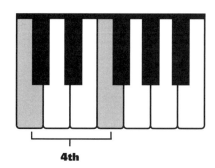

4th

Notice that 4ths are written from **line to space** or **space to line**, like 2nds. You will find that this is true for all even-numbered intervals.

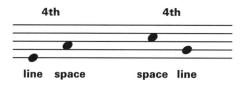

4th   4th

line   space   space   line

Some of the 4ths in this piece are labeled; you label the rest.

Go Fourth and Make Music!

MELODIC 5THS

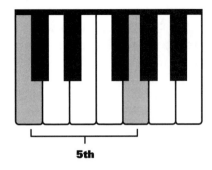

To play a 5th, skip three white keys.

Notice that 5ths are written **line to line** or **space to space**, like 3rds. You will find that this is true for all odd-numbered intervals.

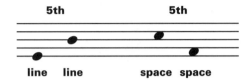

Fifth Avenue

One 5th is labeled in the following piece; you label the rest.

After more than four decades, jazz and fusion great Chick Corea continues to enjoy a career that reflects the evolution of contemporary keyboard playing. With such diverse influences as Mozart, Charlie Parker, Beethoven and Bud Powell, his innovations include exciting experimentation with electronic music.

Photo: Courtesy of Chick Corea Productions

HARMONIC 4THS AND 5THS

This exercise has some harmonic 4ths and 5ths, and some harmonic 2nds and 3rds appear in the third and fourth measures. At the end of the exercise is a repeat sign, which means to go back to the beginning and play the exercise again.

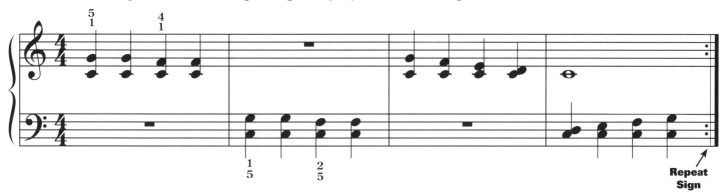

Repeat Sign

Enjoy playing this popular winter song that uses harmonic intervals in the left hand.

A bell sound would be perfect!

Jingle Bells

James Pierpoint

MIDDLE C POSITION

In middle C position, the first finger of each hand is used to play middle C.
Two new bass clef notes are played by the left hand: A and B.

Here are the important things to remember about middle C position:

- Both thumbs are on middle C.
- The right hand is positioned exactly the same as in C position learned on page 16.
- The left hand has fifth finger on F.

Here is middle C position and the notes on the grand staff.

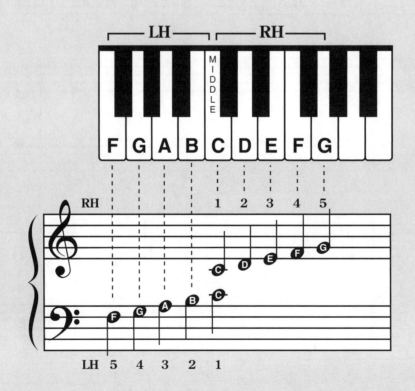

Here's a tune that's played in middle C position. Say the names of the notes aloud as you play until the bass clef A and B notes are fully learned.

Middle C Rock

Whether blues, rock, country, or gospel, Ray Charles mastered them all. His versatility and command of the keyboard made this legendary singer, songwriter and composer one of the most popular entertainers of all time.

Photo: Robert Knight

THE FLAT SIGN

A *flat sign* ♭ before a note means to play the next key
to the left, whether it is a black key or a white key.

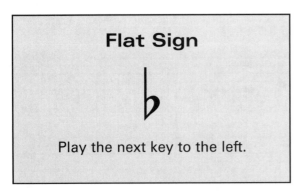

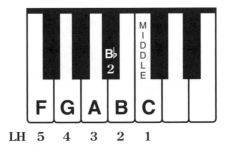

A flat sign is one of several symbols that are called *accidentals*. When an accidental appears before a note, it applies to that note for the rest of the measure. If the accidental does not appear again in the next measure, the note in question returns to its natural position.

This tune is played in middle C position and includes some flat notes.

Try an organ sound for this bluesy tune.

B Flat, B Blue

These pieces will give you some more practice reading flats in middle C position.

Walk in the Park

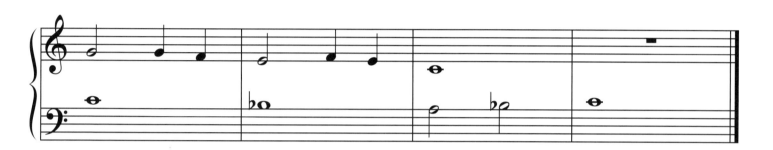

Rockin' All Night Long

G POSITION

G position introduces several new notes: low B, low A, and low G in bass clef
for the left hand and A, B, high C, and high D in treble clef for the right hand.

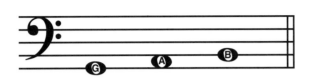 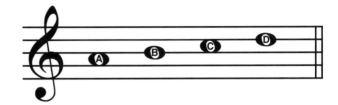

Here is G position and the notes on the grand staff.

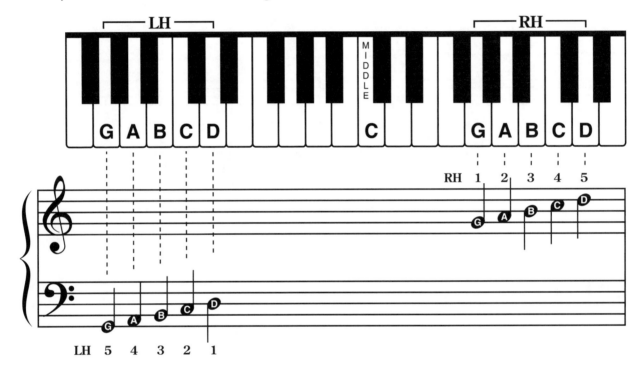

Practice playing the notes in G position, reciting the names of the notes aloud as you play.

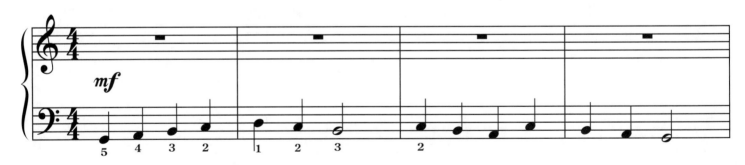

HARMONIC 3RDS, 4THS AND 5THS

This exercise will prepare your left hand to play the next piece. It uses harmonic 3rds, 4ths and 5ths.

Be sure to learn each hand alone before playing hands together. Practice slowly at first.

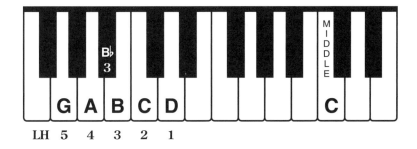

This piece has a definite rock 'n' roll feel, so try one of your keyboard's cool synth sounds. It will also sound great with an electric piano sound.

G Rock

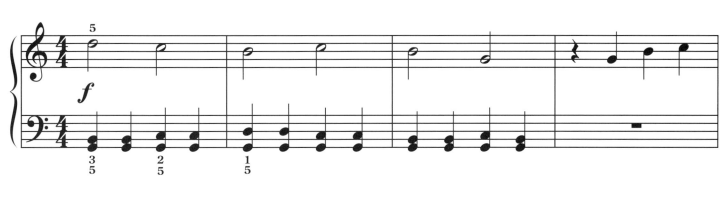

TIED NOTES

A *tie* is a curved line that connects two notes of the same pitch. Two notes connected by a tie are *tied notes*. The second tied note is not struck; rather, the key is held down for the combined values of both notes.

This is a great way to write notes that are longer than one measure...

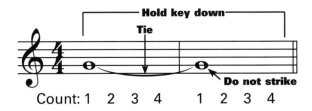

...or to start a long note on the fourth beat of a measure.

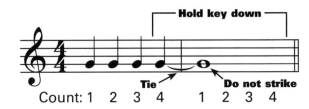

In this C-position exercise, the right hand has notes tied over the bar line into measures 2, 4 and 6. Meanwhile, the left hand plays on the first beat of every measure. Count aloud as you play.

Tie Exercise

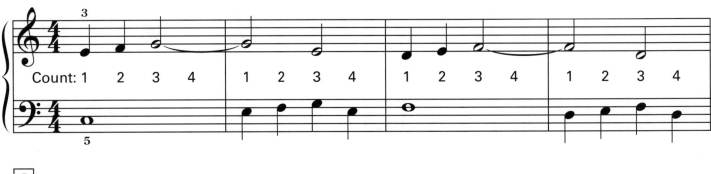

DOTTED HALF NOTES

Adding a dot to the right of a note increases its value by half. Since a half note gets two beats, a dotted half note gets three. A dotted half note is equal to a half note tied to a quarter note.

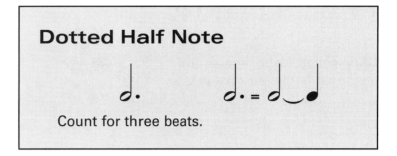

Next New Year's Eve, you can entertain your fellow revelers with this classic tune, which is almost all in C position. In measure 7, reach with your second finger to play E and your hand will be perfectly positioned for your fifth finger to play the A in measure 8 without having to reach. Also, notice that the melody starts in the left hand and moves to the right, then returns to the left hand at the end.

Choose a great holiday sound that will be heard over the merriment, such as brass or string orchestra.

Auld Lang Syne

Traditional Scottish Melody

¾ TIME SIGNATURE

Often called *waltz time*, ¾ time has three beats per measure.

3 A **3** means there are **three** beats in each measure.

4 A **4** means a **quarter note** ♩ gets one beat.

Anna's Waltz

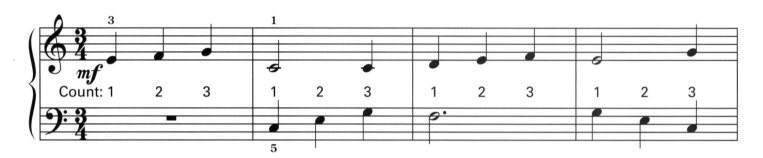

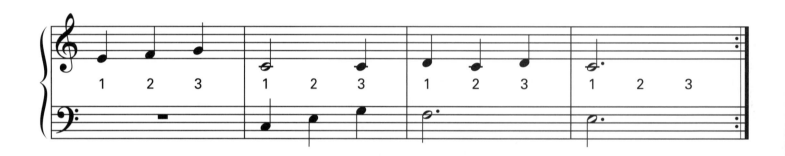

Sarah McLachlan studied classical guitar, piano and voice before signing her first recording contract at the age of 17, and has since become a three-time Grammy Award winner. In 1997, she founded the Lilith Fair, a music tour that focused on female singer/songwriters.

Photo: © Ken Settle

THE NATURAL SIGN

Notice that a *natural sign* is used in the next tune
to indicate a B-natural after a B-flat within the same
measure. A natural sign returns a note that has been
changed by an accidental to its unaltered position.

This bluesy tune uses ties to shift the emphasis off of the strong beats (beats 1 and 3)
and onto the weak beats (beats 2 and 4). This is called *syncopation*.

Tied and True Blues

Try an organ sound with a strong, percussive attack.

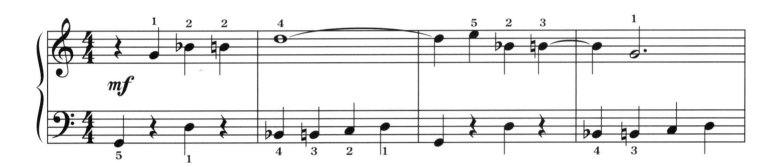

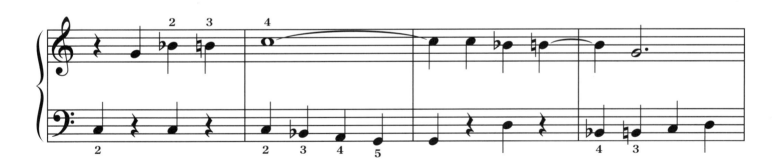

THE C MAJOR CHORD

A *chord* is a combination of three or more notes played together. The *root* of a chord is the note that gives the chord its name. The note C is the root of the *C major chord*, which is made up of the notes C–E–G.

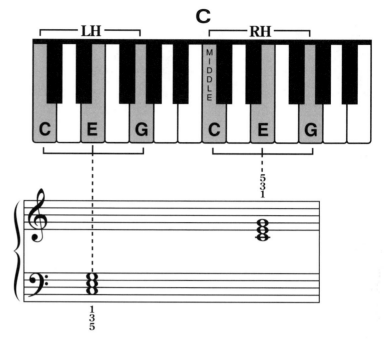

It is very important to play all three notes exactly together, keeping your fingers curved. Practice these C major chords with your left hand.

C Major Chord Warm-up (Left Hand)

Largo
(Theme from the New World Symphony)

Since this melody is from one of the most famous classical symphonies, try it with an orchestral string sound.

Antonin Dvořák

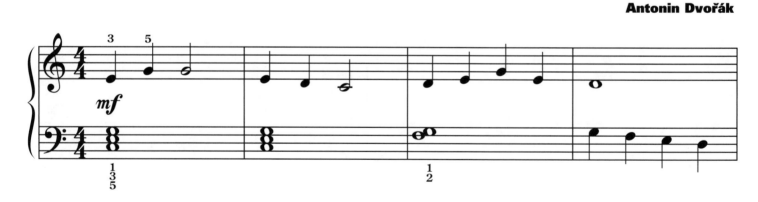

THE PICKUP

When one or more notes are played before the first full measure at the beginning of a piece, it is called a *pickup*. The pickup measure is an *incomplete measure*. Frequently, when a piece begins with a pickup, the last measure will also be incomplete so that the rhythmic values of the two combined equal one full measure.

Practice the C major chord with the right hand before playing "When the Saints Go Marching In."

C Major Chord Warm-up (Right Hand)

When the Saints Go Marching In

"When the Saints Go Marching In" is an American spiritual commonly played by New Orleans Dixieland jazz bands. It will sound great played with a brass sound.

American Spiritual

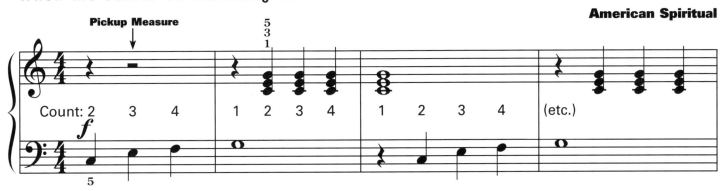

THE G⁷ CHORD

The G⁷ chord is frequently used with the C major chord. Notice that, unlike the C major chord, the root of this chord is not played as the lowest note. This is called an *inversion*.

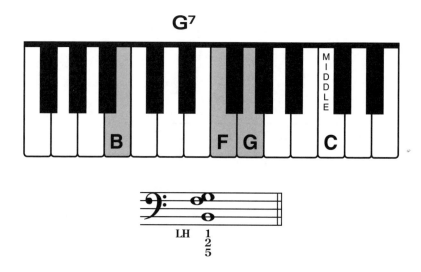

These exercises will help you learn to switch between playing the C and G⁷ chords.

No. 1

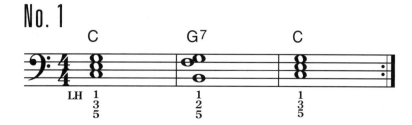

No. 2

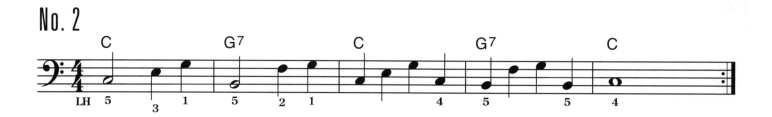

No. 3

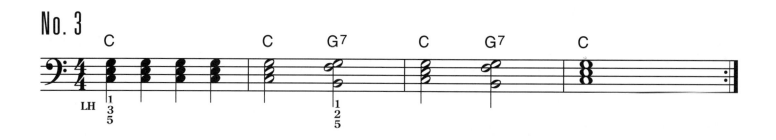

This piece has the melody in the right hand and combines harmonic
2nds and 3rds with chords in the left-hand accompaniment.

Mary Ann

Traditional

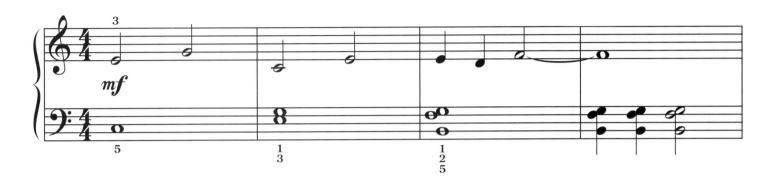

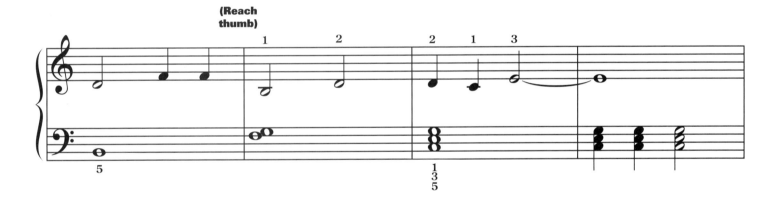

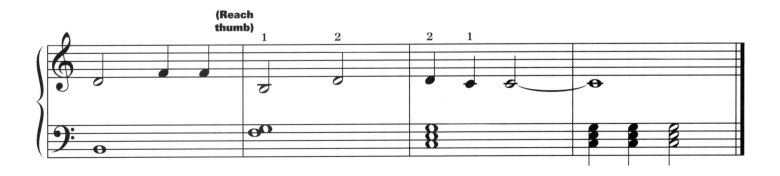

THE F MAJOR CHORD

The *F major chord* often appears with the C major and G7 chords. Like the G7 chord you learned on page 46, the F major chord you will play is an inversion.

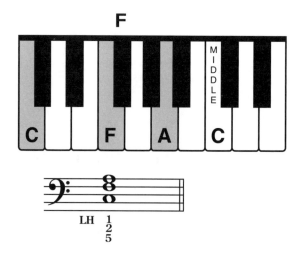

Practicing these exercises will help you learn to play the F major chord in combination with C major and G7.

No. 1

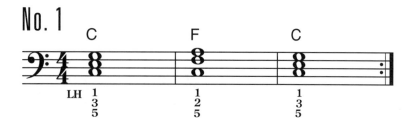

No. 2

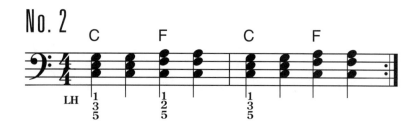

No. 3

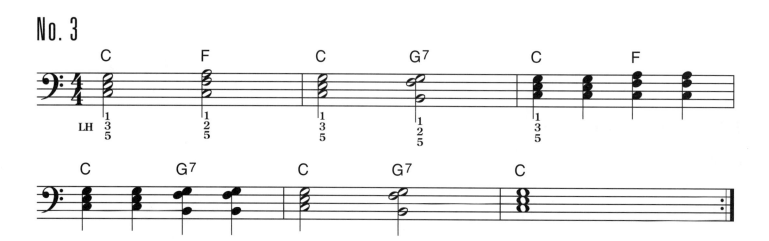

For He's a Jolly Good Fellow

Traditional English Folk Song

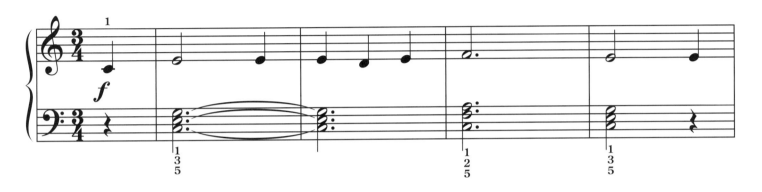

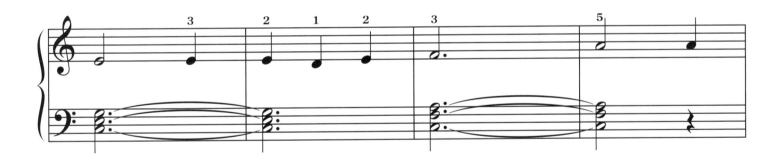

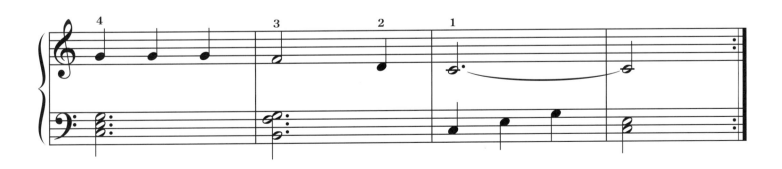

EIGHTH NOTES & EIGHTH RESTS

The duration of an eighth note or eighth rest is one-half beat, which is half as long as a quarter note. Music with eighth notes is counted by dividing the beat into two halves.

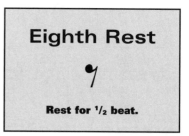

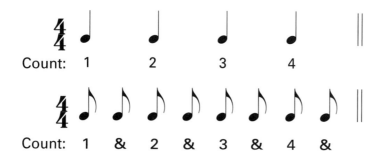

Groups of eighth notes are often connected with beams and grouped into beats. Compare the notes below to the single eighth notes above.

If an eighth note occurs on only one subdivision of a beat, it will usually appear as a single note with a flag. An eighth rest will take the other half of the beat if there is no note.

The following diagram shows the relative values of the types of notes and rests you know so far.

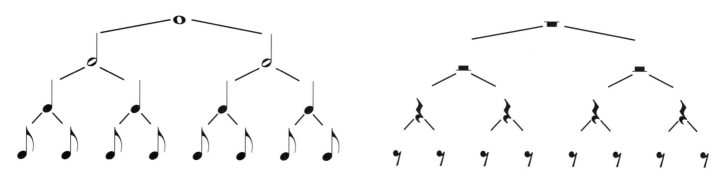

Simple Gifts

Try an organ or string sound for this famous hymn tune.

This piece uses eighth notes in both hands.

Traditional Shaker hymn

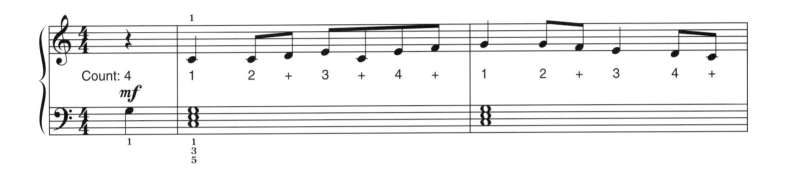

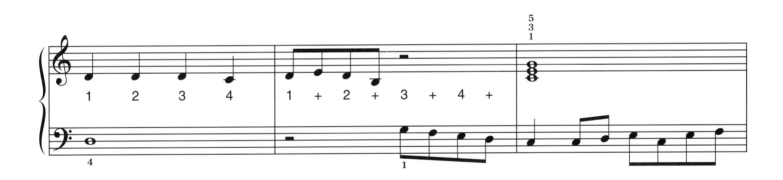

THE SHARP SIGN

A *sharp sign* ♯ before a note means to play the next key to the right, whether it is a black key or a white key. It is an accidental that means the opposite direction of a flat.

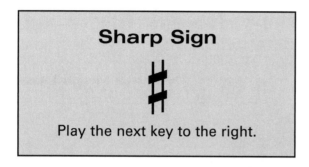

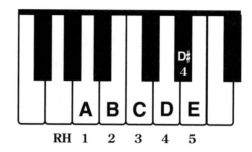

All the rules that apply to flats also apply to sharps: when a sharp appears before a note, it applies to that note for the rest of the measure unless cancelled by a natural sign.

Für Elise

Ludwig van Beethoven

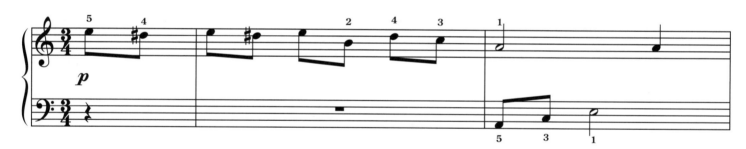

THE DOTTED QUARTER NOTE

A quarter note tied to an eighth note is held for one and a half beats. An eighth note or eighth rest works nicely to take up the other half of the beat:

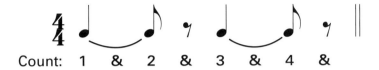

An easier way to show this rhythm is with a *dotted quarter note*. Since a dot increases a note by another half of the note's value, the dotted quarter note is equal to one and a half beats.

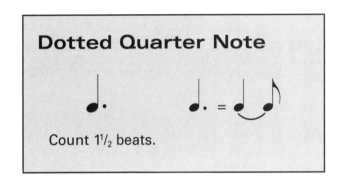

Here are some familiar tunes that use the dotted quarter note rhythm.

London Bridge

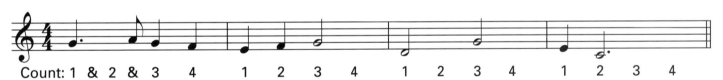

Alouette

Silent Night

Eine Kleine Nachtmusik

Try playing this famous piece for strings with an orchestral string sound.

Wolfgang Amadeus Mozart

Same note, different finger!

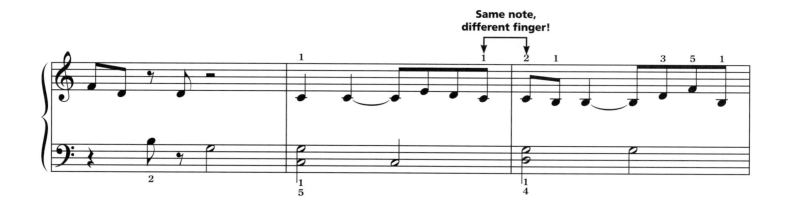

MORE DYNAMIC MARKINGS

Here are some new important dynamic markings:

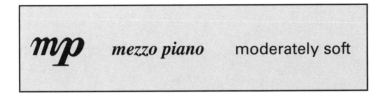

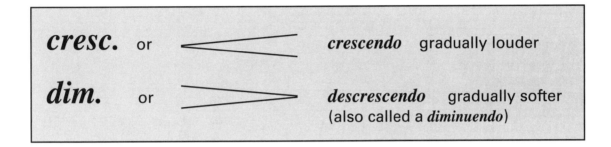

Blue and True

Be sure to play crescendos and decrescendos
as gradual, not sudden, changes in loudness.

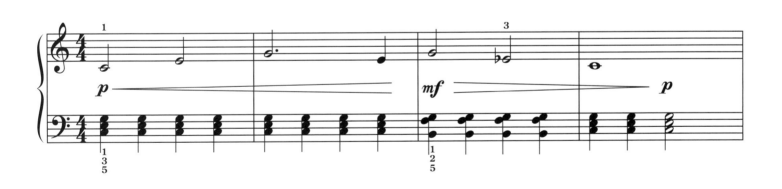

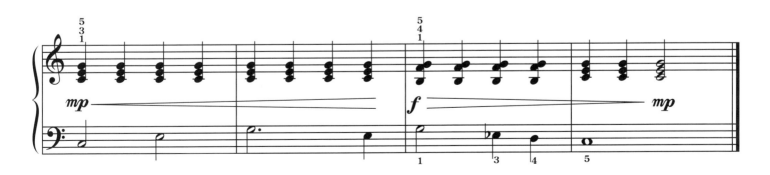

Theme from a Mozart Sonata

Wolfgang Amadeus Mozart

MELODIC & HARMONIC 6THS

To play a 6th, skip four white keys.

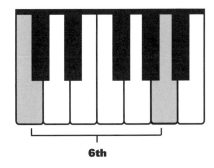

Notice that 6ths are written **line to space** or **space to line**. To reach a 6th, you must reach one key further than a 5-finger position.

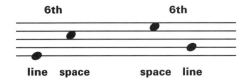

The G7 and F major chords both use 6ths.

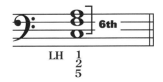
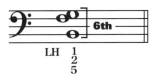

One 6th is labeled in the following piece; you label the rest.

Sixth Sense

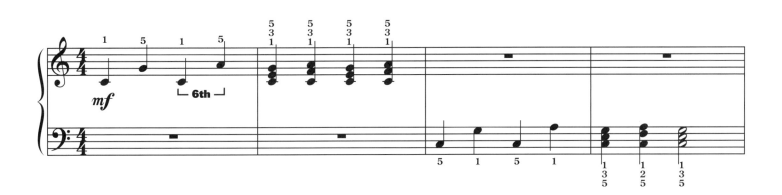

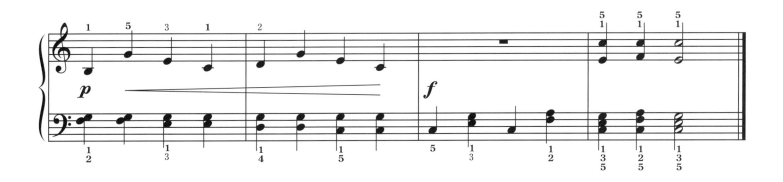

58

MELODIC & HARMONIC 7THS

To play a 7th, skip five white keys.

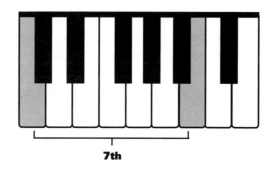

Notice that 7ths are written **line to line** or **space to space**. A 7th spans all the letters of the music alphabet.

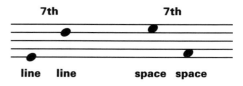

One 7th is labeled in the following piece; you label the rest.

Seventh Heaven

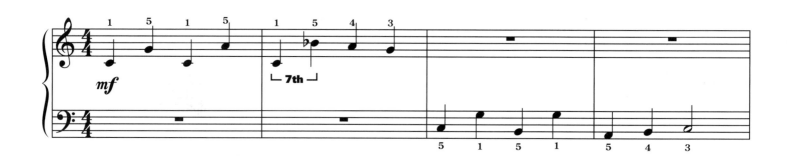

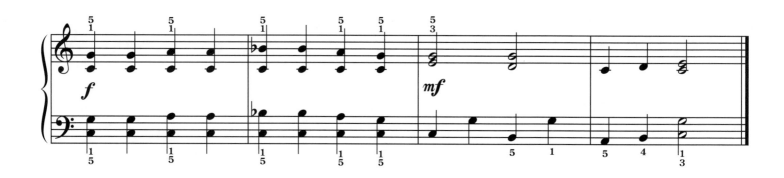

OCTAVES

You can think of an *octave* as an 8th, though it is never called that. An octave is easy to find because it is the distance from one note to the next note of the same name: C to C, D to D, etc.

To play an octave, skip six white keys.

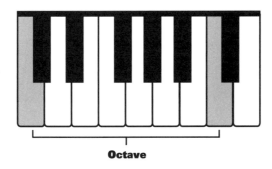

Notice that octaves are written **line to space** or **space to line**. The two notes of an octave always have the same name.

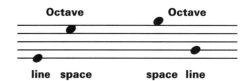

One octave is labeled in the following piece; you label the rest.

Octaboogie

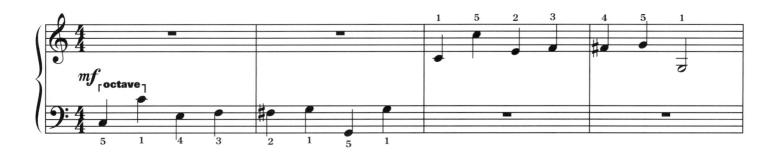

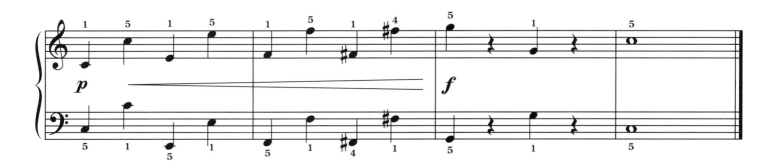

HALF STEPS & WHOLE STEPS

Every piece of music is based on a particular set of notes called a *scale*. In order to understand how this works, we must understand the building blocks of the scale, namely, *whole steps* and *half steps*.

Half Steps

The smallest step is a *half step* (H), which is from one key to the very next key. Natural half steps occur between B & C and E & F; all other half steps are from a white key to a black key, so one of the notes will be a sharp or flat.

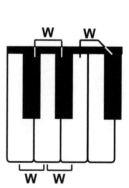

These are all half steps:

Whole Steps

A *whole step* (W) skips over one key. A whole step, in other words, is two half steps. Natural whole steps occur between any two white keys with a black key between them; all other whole steps will have at least one sharp or flat note.

These are all whole steps:

THE KEY OF C MAJOR

The *major scale* is a set of eight notes that follow the pattern W-W-H-W-W-W-H.
Each note of the scale is given a number, called a *degree*.

If you start on the note C and play all the white keys up to the next C,
you've played the *C major scale:* C D E F G A B C.

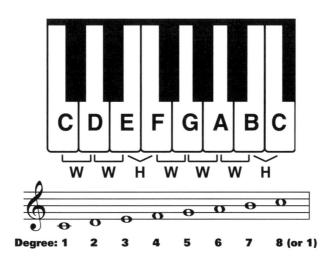

C Major Scale Split

In this exercise, the right hand plays some bass clef notes,
and the left hand plays some treble clef notes.

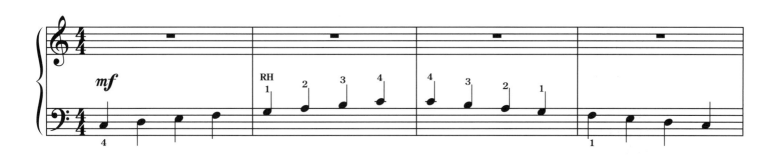

PRACTICING THE C MAJOR SCALE

Because there are eight notes in a scale and only five fingers on each hand, playing an entire scale with one hand requires two finger-crossing techniques that are very important to master.

Thumb Crossing Under

1. Put your right hand in middle C position (thumb on middle C).

2. Press and hold down E with your third finger.

3. As you continue to hold down E, slowly alternate playing C and F with your thumb, passing the thumb under your third finger for the F. It is very important that you **do not twist your wrist.** Keep your fingers curved and your palm open to form a "tunnel" for your thumb; point your thumb into the tunnel to play the F.

4. Perform the same exercise with the left hand in middle C position. Hold down A with your third finger and alternate playing C and G with your thumb, using the same technique described above.

Third Finger Crossing Over

1. Put your right hand in position with thumb on F.

2. Press and hold down F with your thumb.

3. As you continue to hold down F, slowly alternate playing A and E with your third finger, crossing your third finger over your thumb for the E. Again, it is extremely important not to twist your wrist. Use your thumb joint to pivot horizontally over to the E.

4. Perform the same exercise with the left hand in position with thumb on G. Hold down G with your thumb and alternate playing E and A with your third finger, using the same technique described above.

Now we'll put the whole thing together.

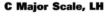

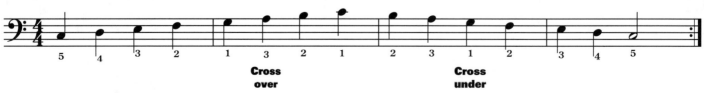

TEMPO MARKINGS

Tempo markings indicate how fast music is played. Like dynamics, many tempo marks are Italian words. Below are three of the most common Italian tempo markings.

Andante	(ahn-DAHN-teh)	slow
Moderato	(mod-deh-RAH-toh)	moderately
Allegro	(ah-LAY-groh)	fast

Scales are great for improving your technical agility. Practice the C major scale exercise below as a warm-up before your daily practice. Repeat the entire exercise three times at each of the indicated tempos. If the fingering is difficult when you play hands together, spend extra time practicing just that spot until it is easy, then go back and play the whole exercise from the beginning.

Note: On the DVD, the scale is played only once at each tempo.

C Major Scale Exercise

Andante (3 times)
Moderato (3 times)
Allegro (3 times)

ARTICULATION

Music notation uses a variety of symbols that tell the performer exactly how to play
a piece of music so that it sounds as the composer intended. Dynamics and tempo
markings, for example, tell how loud and how fast to play. Other symbols, called
articulations, give even more specific instructions about how to play the notes.
For example, notes can be played smoothly connected, like the calm flow of a river,
or notes can be played separate and detached from one another, like the sound
of falling raindrops. Articulations are details that give music life and character,
so always follow them carefully.

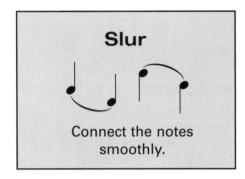

Slur

Connect the notes
smoothly.

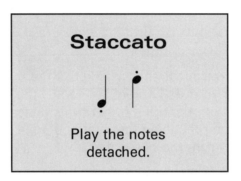

Staccato

Play the notes
detached.

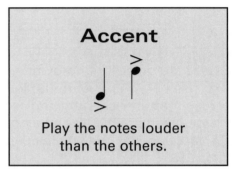

Accent

Play the notes louder
than the others.

Note: Don't confuse a slur with a tie. A tie will always connect two of the same
note, and a slur will connect two different notes *or* several notes together.

Slide, Bounce, and Bang

Be sure to play all the slurs, staccatos, and accents correctly.
Try to play them correctly even the first time you practice the piece.

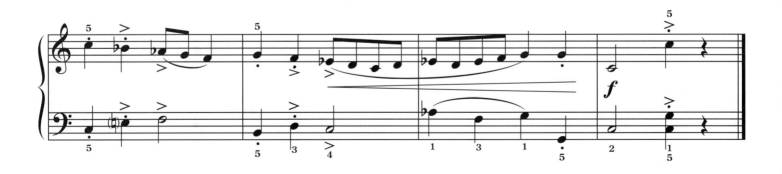

RITARDANDOS & FERMATAS

The marking *ritardando* means to gradually slow down. The direction *a tempo* tells you to return to the normal tempo. It is important to slow down gradually for a ritardando rather than simply becoming suddenly slower. Think of it as a car coming gradually to a stop rather than a car hitting a brick wall.

rit. or *ritard.*	gradually slower
a tempo	return to the normal tempo

A *fermata* means to pause. Notes with a fermata should be held about twice as long as normal.

Fermata

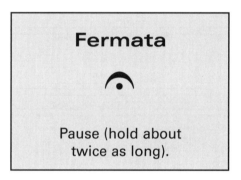

Pause (hold about twice as long).

Good Morning to You

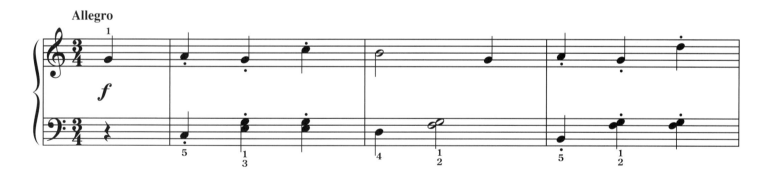

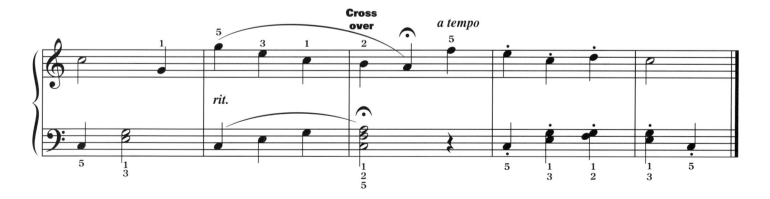

66

$\frac{2}{4}$ TIME SIGNATURE

A **2** means there are **two** beats in each measure.

A **4** means a **quarter note** ♩ gets one beat.

Slur to Staccato

Connect, then lift off.

Russian Folk Dance

The two-note slur with a staccato has a characteristic "down-up" sound. This is accomplished by allowing the wrist to dip loosely for the first note, then lift up for the second note. Be sure to keep the wrist relaxed.

Ludwig van Beethoven

When you get to the end, repeat from here, not the beginning.

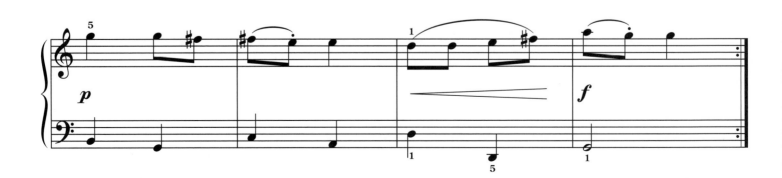

PRIMARY CHORDS

Although accidentals occur frequently in music, most pieces stick to the notes of one particular scale, which gives the music a sense of unity and direction. This concept of a scale providing a sort of musical "home base" is known as being *in a key*. For example, a piece that is composed using the C major scale is in the *key of C major*.

As you know, a *chord* is a combination of three or more notes played together. You also learned that the *root* of a chord is the note that gives the chord its name; C is the root of a C major chord, F is the root of an F major chord, and so on.

Triads

A *triad* is a chord with three notes: the root, a third above the root, and a fifth above the root. Let's take a look at the triads that can be formed using each note of the C major scale as a root.

In the diagram below, a triad has been built on each degree of the scale. Three of these triads, those built on the 1st, 4th, and 5th degrees of the scale (see page 61), are especially important and are called the *primary triads.* Notice the Roman numerals below the corresponding scale degree numbers—these can be used to refer to the chords of the scale. For example, the triad built on the 1st degree is called the I chord ("one" chord), the triad built on the 4th degree is the IV chord ("four" chord), and the triad on the 5th degree is the V chord ("five" chord). The primary triads, I, IV & V, are the three most functional, or useful, chords in any key. In the key of C, the primary chords are C major, F major, and G major.

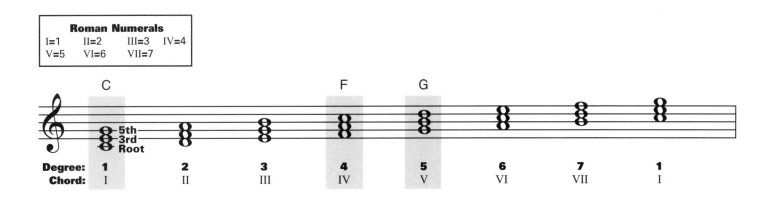

The arrangement of chords in a particular order is called a *progression*. Play the example below and listen carefully. As you hold the notes of the V chord, try to imagine what the I chord will sound like. It sounds like the music wants to return to the I chord in order to be finished.

Primary Progression

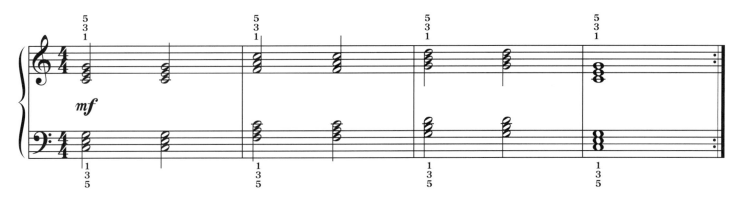

CHORD INVERSIONS

Let's take a look at how the familiar inversions of the chords you already know are derived.

The C, F, and G major triads on the previous page are in *root position*, meaning the root note is the lowest note of the chord. In Book 1, you learned an inversion of the F chord and an inversion of a type of G chord called a G7 chord. Where does the "7" come from in a G7 chord? It is simply an added note, an interval of a 7th above the root. The complete G7 chord, then, actually has four notes, though often only the root, 3rd, and 7th are played.

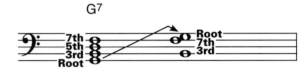

Primary Chords in the Key of C Major

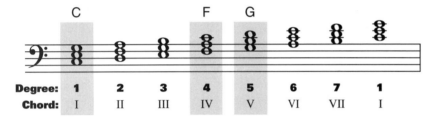

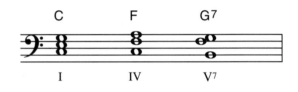

Degree:	1	2	3	4	5	6	7	1
Chord:	I	II	III	IV	V	VI	VII	I

The following example features the primary chords in root position, followed by the same progression using inversions. Notice how the inversions make the progression easier to play on the keyboard.

Solid State

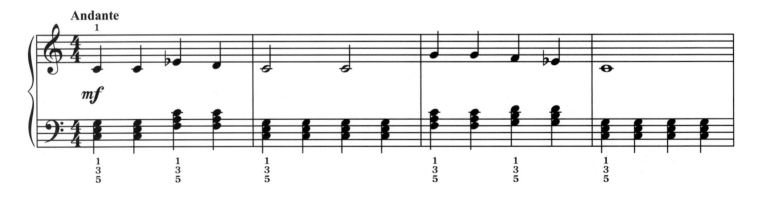

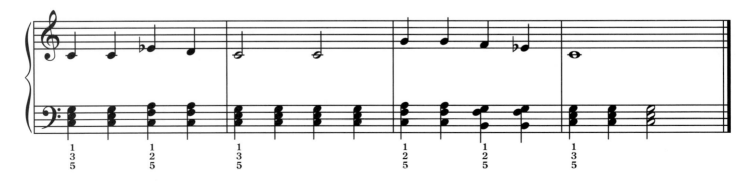

THE SUSTAIN PEDAL (DAMPER PEDAL)

Most pianos have two or three pedals. The pedal on the far right is the *damper pedal*, which, when depressed, lifts all the felt dampers off of the piano strings to allow the notes to ring. Electronic keyboards are typically equipped with a *sustain pedal* that creates the same effect as the piano's damper pedal. (The term "sustain pedal" will be used in this book to mean either pedal.)

Using the sustain pedal can add color and life to keyboard music. When pressed down, the pedal is "on." Because the notes continue to ring after you've lifted your fingers off the keys, it becomes possible to create a rich wash of harmony. To turn the pedal "off" and silence the notes, simply lift it up. Turning the pedal off and then immediately back on again is called *changing* the pedal. When playing music with sustain pedal, it is important to change the pedal appropriately in order to avoid creating a muddy mess of notes that aren't supposed to be heard at the same time. Always use your ears to be sure you aren't overdoing it.

In classical keyboard music, pedal markings are usually very specific and indicate exactly when to depress and release, as shown in the example below.

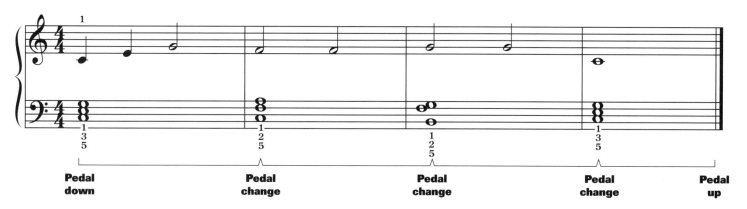

Sometimes, the abbreviation 𝄢ℰ𝒹. is used to show where the pedal should be pressed or changed. In this case, the symbol ✳ is used whenever the pedal should be taken off completely.

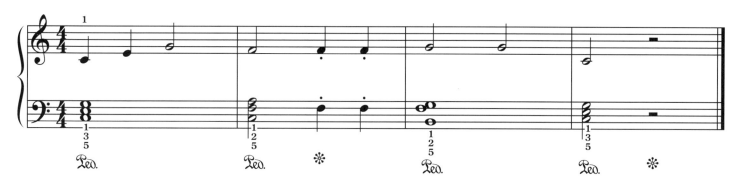

Important: In a lot of keyboard music, especially popular music, specific pedal on and off markings are not shown. Instead, the words "with pedal" might be seen under the first measure. In many cases, no indication whatsoever will be given; this does not necessarily mean pedal should not be used—it is simply being left to the discretion of the performer. Use your ears to decide what is best. (Hint: In most cases, you will want to change the pedal at least at the start of each measure.)

Bach Prelude in C

This famous prelude was used by Charles Gounod as the basis for the famous Bach/Gounod "Ave Maria." Follow the pedal markings carefully.

Johann Sebastian Bach

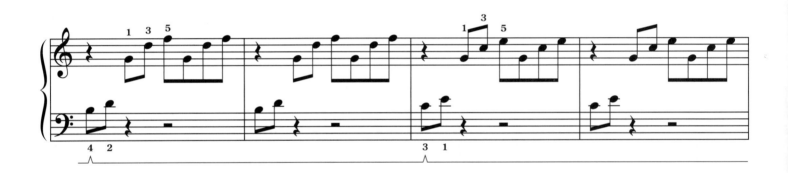

THE KEY OF G MAJOR

The G major scale contains one sharp, F♯. A piece of music based on the G major scale is said to be in the *key of G major.*

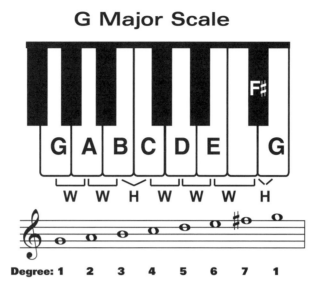

G Major Scale

Practice the G major scale right hand alone, then left hand alone, then hands together three times at each of the indicated tempos. The fingering is the same as for the C major scale.

Note: On the DVD, the scale is played only once at each tempo.

Andante (RH, LH, together 3 times)
Moderato (RH, LH, together 3 times)
Allegro (RH, LH, together 3 times)

Primary Chords in the Key of G Major

THE KEY SIGNATURE

A *key signature* indicates notes that will be sharp or flat throughout a piece of music. For example, music in the key of G major contains F#. Rather than using accidentals to change all the F's in the music to F#'s, the sharp can be placed in the key signature at the beginning of every staff.

Key Signature of G Major

Both lines of "All Through the Night" below will sound exactly alike.
Line 1 uses accidentals, and Line 2 uses a key signature.

All Through the Night

Line 1

Line 2

Minuet in G

Notice the key signature! Play every F as an F♯.

Play this piece with a piano
or harpsichord sound.

Johann Sebastian Bach

A PIECE IN TWO KEYS

Here is a tune by Leopold Mozart, the father of Wolfgang Amadeus Mozart.
It is first shown in the key of C major, then in the key of G major. Playing the
same music in a different key is called *transposing.*

Burleske

Key of C

Leopold Mozart

Key of G

Alouette

Play this French tune with an
accordion sound for fun!

French folk song

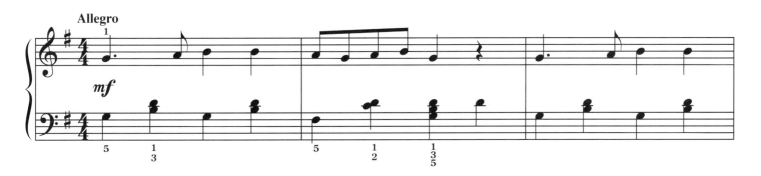

TEMPO & EXPRESSION

Tempo markings, dynamics, and other changes in music create *expression*. Like dynamic signs, many tempo marks and other musical directions are Italian words.

Below are the most common Italian tempo markings and their meanings. Be sure to memorize them.

Largo	(LAHR-goh)	Very slow
Adagio	(ah-DAH-joh)	Slow
Andante	(ahn-DAHN-teh)	Moderately slow, walking speed
Moderato	(moh-deh-RAH-toh)	Moderately
Allegretto	(ahl-leh-GREH-toh)	Moderately fast
Allegro	(ahl-LAY-groh)	Fast
Presto	(PRES-toh)	Very fast

Other Italian words are often used to further indicate tempo, character, or feeling. Here are some of the more common ones you might see.

dolce	(DOHL-cheh)	Sweetly
subito	(SOO-bee-toh)	Suddenly, as in *subito p* (suddenly soft)
legato	(leh-GAH-toh)	Smooth
staccato	(stah-KAH-toh)	Detached
marcato	(mar-KAH-toh)	Heavily accented (sometimes indicated by the symbol ʌ)
molto	(MOHL-toh)	Very, as in *molto legato* (very smooth)
poco	(POH-koh)	Little, as in *poco dim.* (little diminuendo)
simile	(SEE-mee-leh)	In the same manner, as in *pedal simile* (continue the same pedal pattern)

Here's a handy chart of dynamic signs. Some you already know, others are new.

ppp	pianississimo	(pyah-nees-SEES-see-moh)	Very, very soft
pp	pianissimo	(pyah-NEES-see-moh)	Very soft
p	piano	(PYAH-noh)	Soft
mp	mezzo piano	(MED-zoh PYAH-noh)	Moderately soft
mf	mezzo forte	(MED-zoh FOHR-teh)	Moderately loud
f	forte	(FOHR-teh)	Loud
ff	fortissimo	(fohr-TEES-see-moh)	Very loud
fff	fortississimo	(fohr-tees-SEES-see-moh)	Very, very loud

Remember: The more expression you put into your playing, the more skilled you will sound as a performer. So follow all the signs and symbols in the written music!

TRIPLETS

A *triplet* is three notes played in the time of two. An eighth-note triplet is three eighth notes played in one beat. The notes of an eighth-note triplet appear beamed together with a small number 3.

Eighth-Note Triplet

Play three eighth notes in one beat.

Count 1 & a

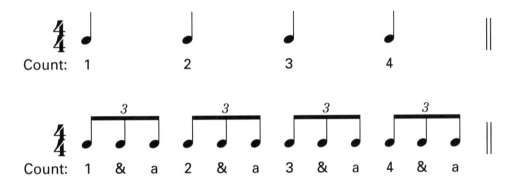

Beautiful Dreamer

Count carefully!

 TIME SIGNATURE

In $\frac{6}{8}$ time, the eighth note, not the quarter note, receives one beat.

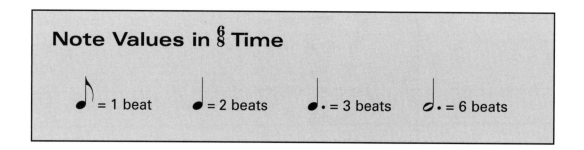

A **6** means there are **six** beats in each measure.

An **8** means an **eighth note** ♪ gets one beat.

Note Values in $\frac{6}{8}$ Time

♪ = 1 beat   ♩ = 2 beats   ♩. = 3 beats   ♩. = 6 beats

Music in this time signature is felt with two strong pulses: on beat 1 and beat 4.
Below are some common rhythmic groupings.

Count: **1** 2 3 **4** 5 6   **1** 2 3 **4** 5 6   **1** 2 3 **4** 5 6   **1** 2 3 **4** 5 6

Alphabeats

The Irish Washerwoman

Traditional Irish tune

THE KEY OF F MAJOR

The F major scale contains one flat, B♭. A piece of music based
on the F major scale is said to be in the *key of F major.*

F Major Scale

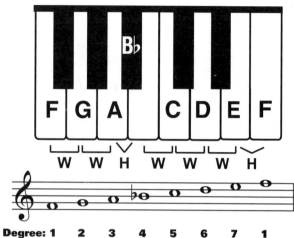

Degree: 1   2   3   4   5   6   7   1

Key Signature of F Major

F Major Scale

Notice the different fingering in the right hand. Because of the placement of the
black key in the scale, the thumb must cross under the fourth finger rather than
the third finger. Remember to play every B as B♭ because of the key signature.

Note: On the DVD, the scale is played only once at each tempo.

Andante (RH, LH, together 3 times)
Moderato (RH, LH, together 3 times)
Allegro (RH, LH, together 3 times)

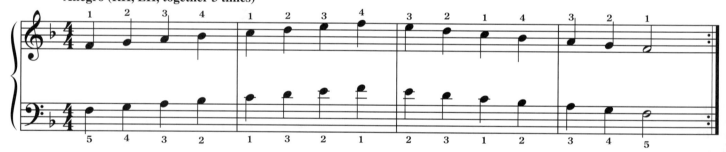

Primary Chords in the Key of F Major

Joy to the World

Follow all the dynamics and articulations to make this holiday
favorite fun and exciting! Remember to observe the key signature.

*Try playing with a
festive brass sound!*

Traditional

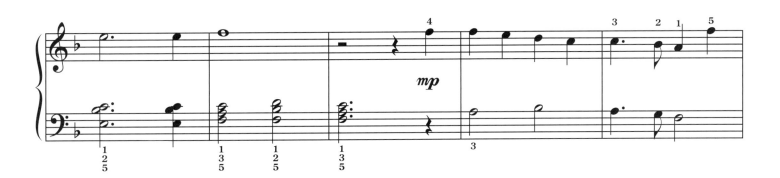

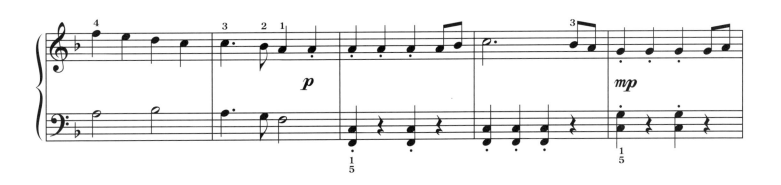

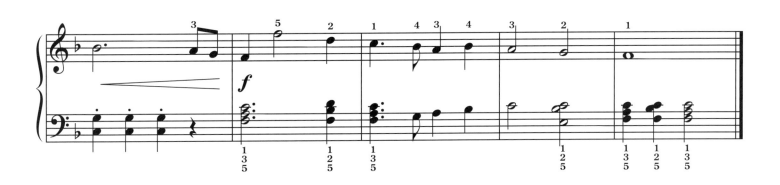

A PIECE IN THREE KEYS

Here we have a tune written in each of the three keys
you've learned: C, G, and F. Follow the key signatures.

Three-Key Rock

Key of C

Key of G

Key of F

REPEATS

In music notation, there are several ways to show when some or all of the music should simply be repeated the same way. You have already learned about repeat dots, which tell you to go back to the beginning of the music or back to repeat dots facing the other way. Here are some of the more elaborate repeat signs.

1st and 2nd Endings
On the repeat, skip the 1st ending and play the 2nd ending instead.

Ode to Joy (Beethoven)

D.C. al Fine
D.C. stands for *da capo*, which means the beginning. *Fine* means the end.
When you see D.C. al Fine, go back to the beginning and play to the *Fine* sign.

Au Claire de la Lune (French folk tune)

D.S. al Fine
D.S. stands for *dal segno*, which refers to the sign 𝄋.

When you see D.S. al Fine, go back to the 𝄋 and play to the *Fine* sign.

The Marines' Hymn (U.S. Marine Corps)

MINOR KEYS

A *minor* sound has a different quality than a *major* sound. Minor sounds are often considered dark, moody, or somber, whereas major sounds have a bright and cheerful feel.

For every major scale, there is a *minor* scale that contains the same notes and therefore uses the same key signature. The notes of the minor scale can be played by starting and ending on the sixth degree of a major scale. For example, playing all the white keys from C to C is a C major scale, but starting and ending on A gives you the A minor scale. Because of its close relationship to the major scale, it is known as the *relative minor*.

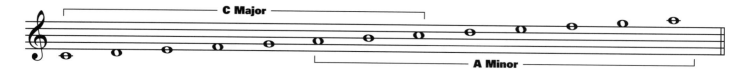

Below are the three major scales you know and their relative minor scales. These minor scales are known as *natural minor* because they contain the exact same notes as the relative major scale.

Practice these scales daily. Play the right hand alone, then left hand alone, then hands together three times Andante, then Moderato, then Allegro.

Major Scale

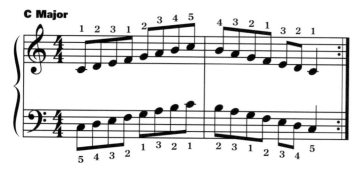

Relative Minor Scale

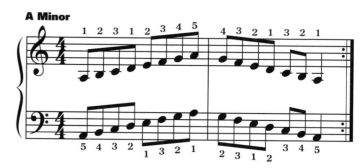

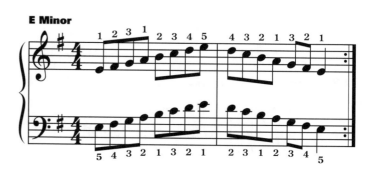

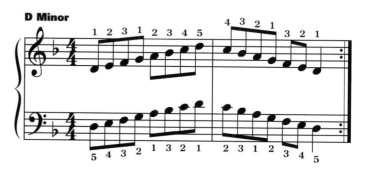

Scherzo

This example begins in A minor and then changes to the relative major, C.
Listen to how the character of the music changes.

Carl Maria von Weber

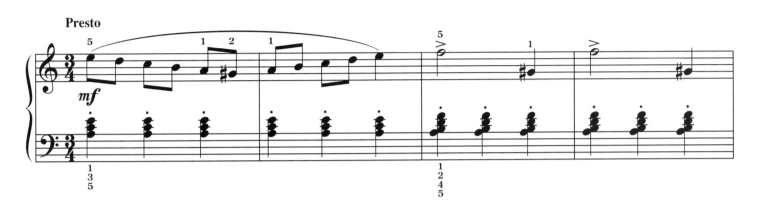

HARMONIC MINOR

The *harmonic minor scale* is a form of the minor scale in which the seventh degree is raised a half step.

Below are the harmonic minor forms of the A minor, D minor, and E minor scales. Notice that the raised seventh step is written with an accidental and not put in the key signature.

Practice these scales as the others, playing just right hand, then just left hand, then hands together, three times Andante, Moderato, then Allegro.

A Harmonic Minor

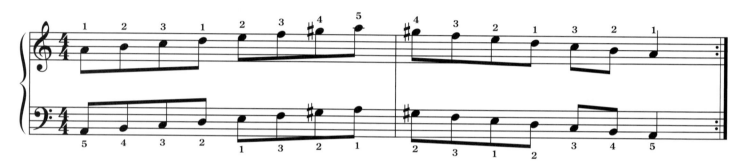

D Harmonic Minor

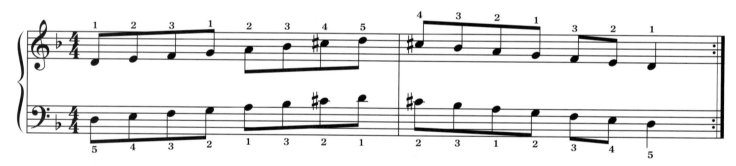

E Harmonic Minor

Primary Chords in Minor Keys

For music in a minor key, the chords are built using the notes of the harmonic minor scale. The concept is the same as for the major scale: the primary triads are I, IV, and V. The I and IV chords in a minor key are *minor triads.* The V chord is usually played as a V7, just like in a major key.

Triads in A Minor

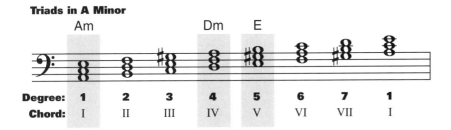

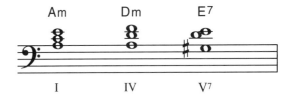

Triads in E Minor

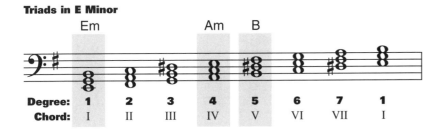

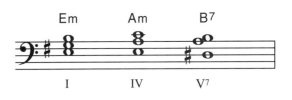

Triads in D Minor

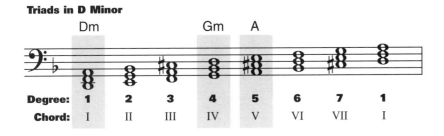

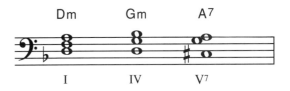

Symphony No. 40

A *coda* is an ending. When you see D.C. al Coda, go back to the beginning
and play until you see *To Coda*, then skip to the coda marked by the symbol ⊕.

Notice the key signature: Does this piece sound like it is in G major, or the
relative minor, E minor? (The answer is at the bottom.)

Wolfgang Amadeus Mozart

E minor

Waves of the Danube

Here's a piece with a key signature of one flat. Can you tell if it is F major or its relative minor, D minor? (The answer is at the bottom of the page.)

This tune is frequently played at anniversary celebrations.

Ion Ivanovici

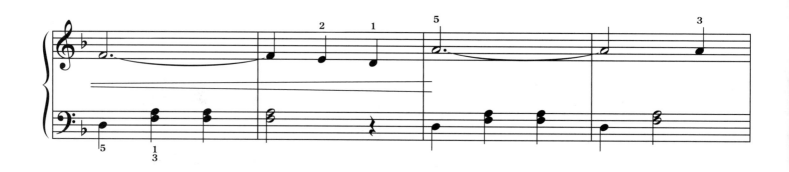

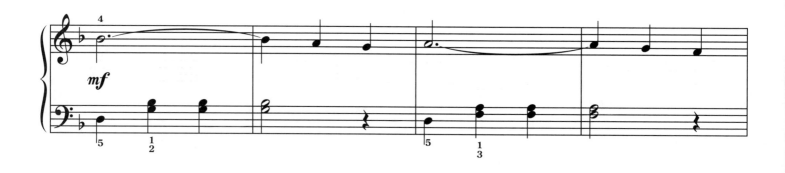

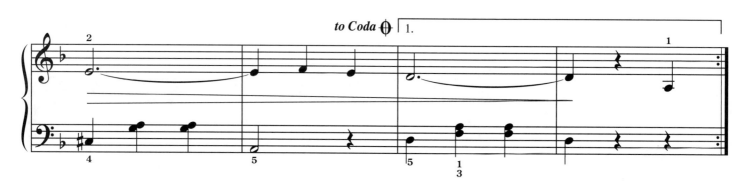

The Entertainer

Congratulations! You're about to play an arrangement of one of the most popular pieces of keyboard music ever written. Be sure to follow all the dynamics and articulations to make this ragtime classic come alive!

Play this Joplin favorite with a honky-tonk piano sound!

Scott Joplin

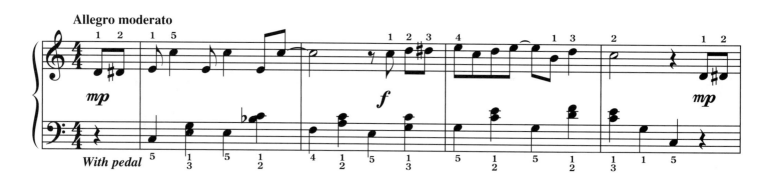

CHORD REFERENCE

Major
A

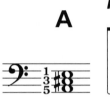

Minor
Am

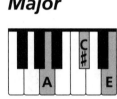

Diminished
A°

Augmented
A⁺

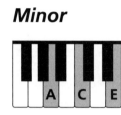

Major 7th
Amaj⁷

Dominant 7th
A⁷

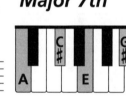

Minor 7th
Am⁷

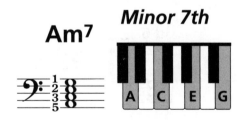

Diminished 7th
A°⁷

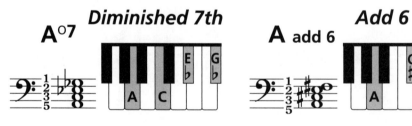

Add 6
A add 6

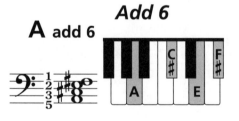

A♯

A♯ *Major*

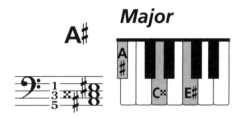

A♯m *Minor*

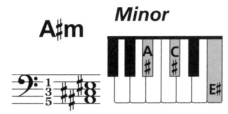

A♯○ *Diminished*

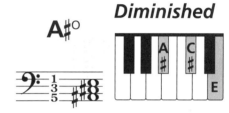

A♯+ *Augmented*

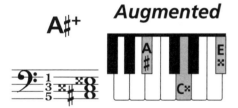

A♯maj⁷ *Major 7th*

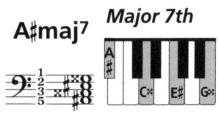

A♯7 *Dominant 7th*

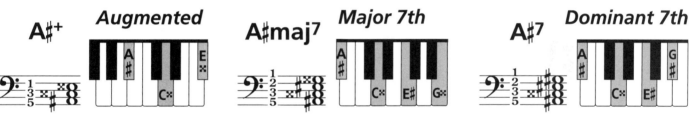

A♯m⁷ *Minor 7th*

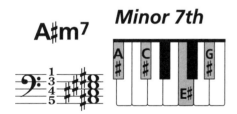

A♯○7 *Diminished 7th*

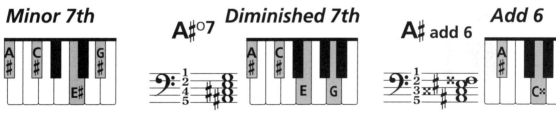

A♯ add 6 *Add 6*

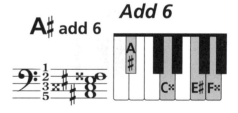

B♭

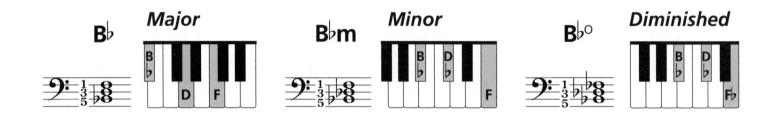

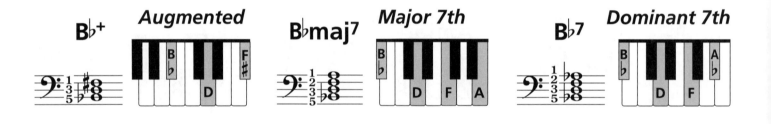

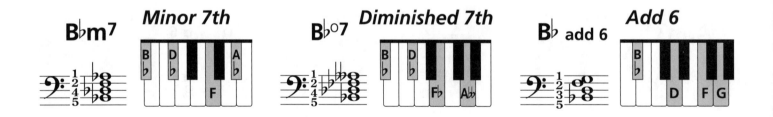

B

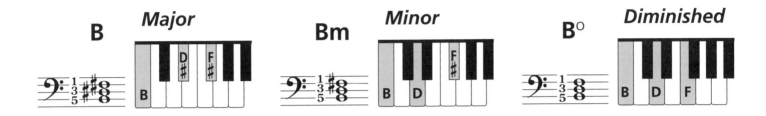

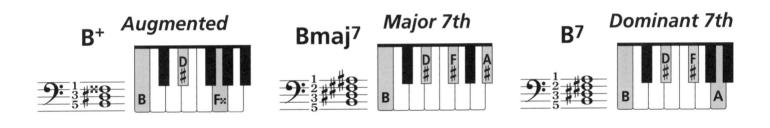

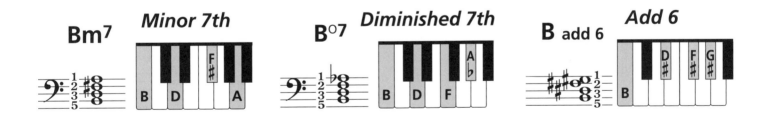

C

C — *Major*

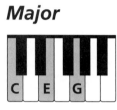

Cm — *Minor*

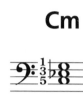
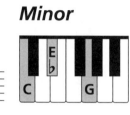

C° — *Diminished*

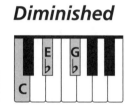

C⁺ — *Augmented*

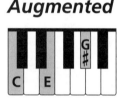

Cmaj⁷ — *Major 7th*

C⁷ — *Dominant 7th*

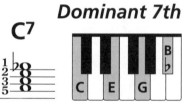

Cm⁷ — *Minor 7th*

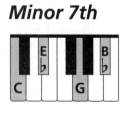

C°⁷ — *Diminished 7th*

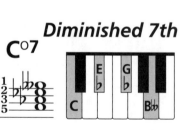

C add 6 — *Add 6*

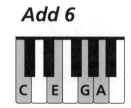

C♯

Major

C♯

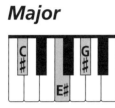

Minor

C♯m

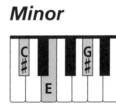

Diminished

C♯°

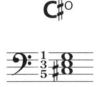
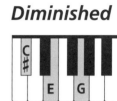

Augmented

C♯+

Major 7th

C♯maj⁷

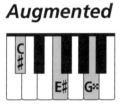

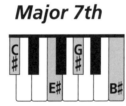

Dominant 7th

C♯7

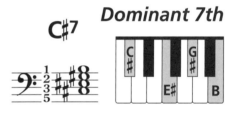

Minor 7th

C♯m⁷

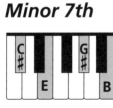

Diminished 7th

C♯°7

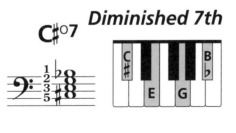

Add 6

C♯ add 6

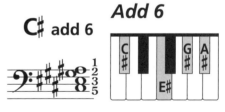

D♭

D♭ *Major*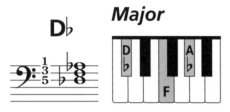

D♭m *Minor*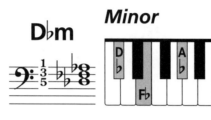

D♭° *Diminished*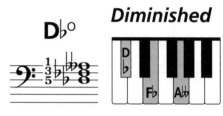

D♭+ *Augmented*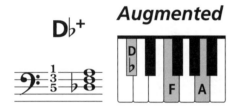

D♭maj7 *Major 7th*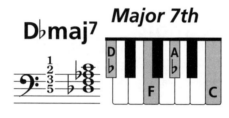

D♭7 *Dominant 7th*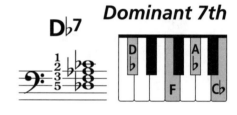

D♭m7 *Minor 7th*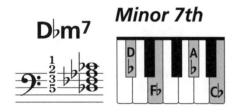

D♭°7 *Diminished 7th*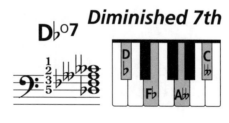

D♭ add 6 *Add 6*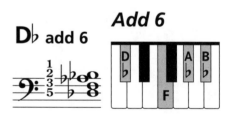

D

Major

D

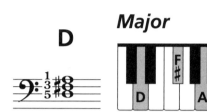

Minor

Dm

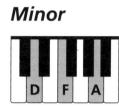

Diminished

D°

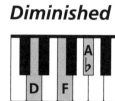

Augmented

D⁺

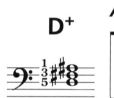
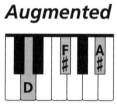

Major 7th

Dmaj⁷

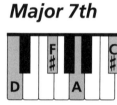

Dominant 7th

D⁷

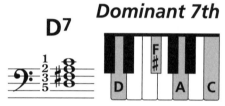

Minor 7th

Dm⁷

Diminished 7th

D°⁷

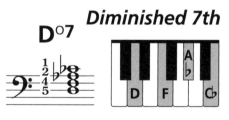

Add 6

D add 6

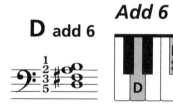

D#

D# — *Major*
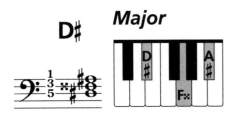

D#m — *Minor*
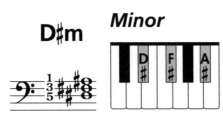

D#° — *Diminished*
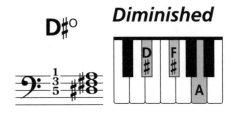

D#+ — *Augmented*
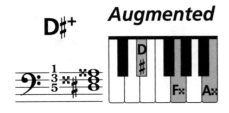

D#maj7 — *Major 7th*
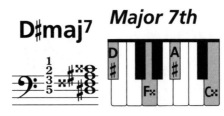

D#7 — *Dominant 7th*
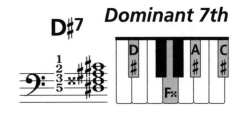

D#m7 — *Minor 7th*
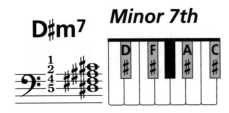

D#°7 — *Diminished 7th*
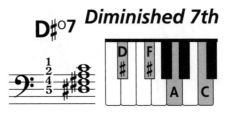

D# add 6 — *Add 6*
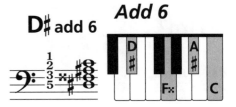

Eb

Major

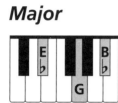

Minor

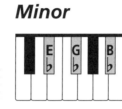

Diminished

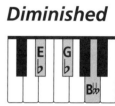

Augmented

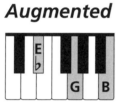

Major 7th

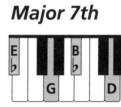

Dominant 7th
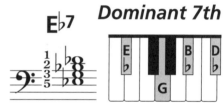

Minor 7th

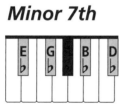

Diminished 7th
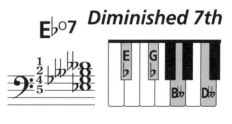

Add 6
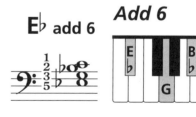

E

Major
E

Minor
Em

Diminished
E°
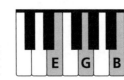

Augmented
E+
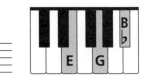

Major 7th
Emaj7
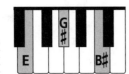

Dominant 7th
E7

Minor 7th
Em7
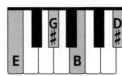

Diminished 7th
E°7

Add 6
E add 6
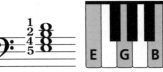

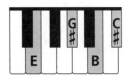

F

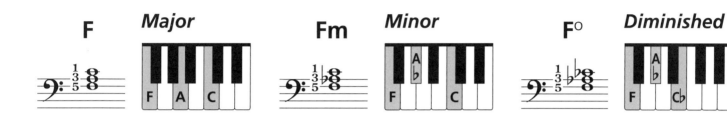

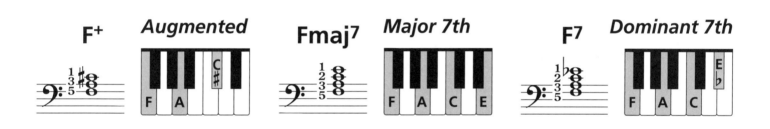

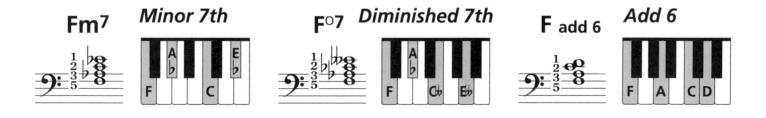

F#

F# *Major*

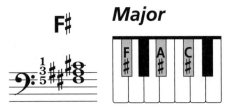

F#m *Minor*

F#° *Diminished*

F#+ *Augmented*

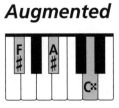

F#maj⁷ *Major 7th*

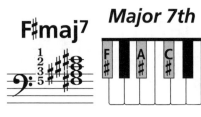

F#7 *Dominant 7th*

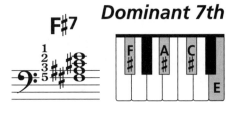

F#m⁷ *Minor 7th*

F#°7 *Diminished 7th*

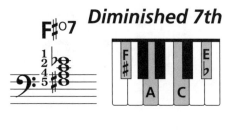

F# add 6 *Add 6*

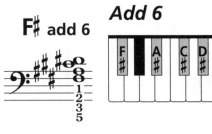

G♭

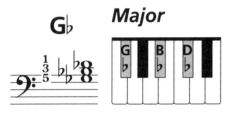

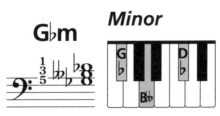

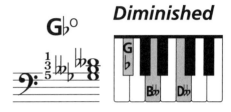

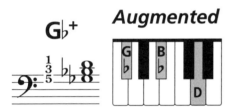

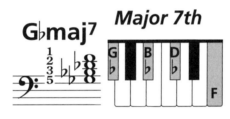

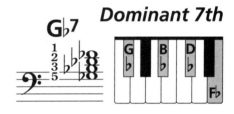

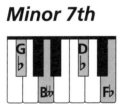

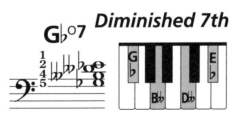

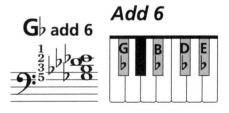

G

G *Major*
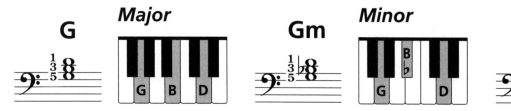

Gm *Minor*

G° *Diminished*
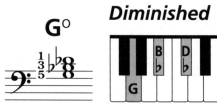

G⁺ *Augmented*
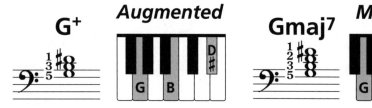

Gmaj⁷ *Major 7th*

G⁷ *Dominant 7th*
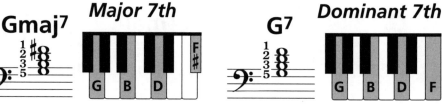

Gm⁷ *Minor 7th*
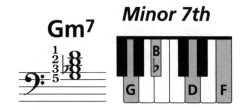

G°7 *Diminished 7th*
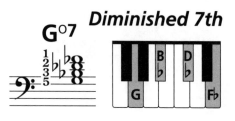

G add 6 *Add 6*
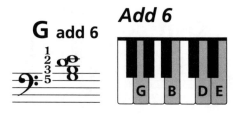

G#

Major

G#

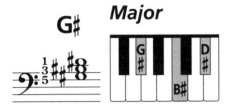

Minor

G#m

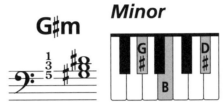

Diminished

G#°

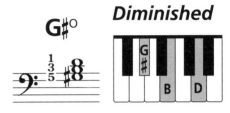

Augmented

G#+

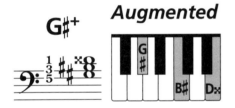

Major 7th

G#maj⁷

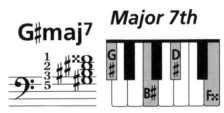

Dominant 7th

G#7

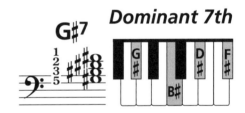

Minor 7th

G#m⁷

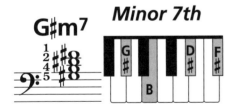

Diminished 7th

G#°7

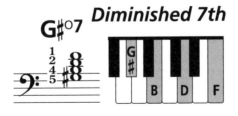

Add 6

G# add 6

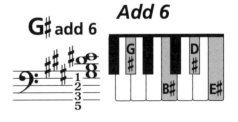

Major
A♭

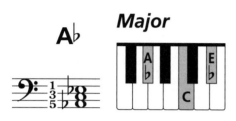

Minor
A♭m

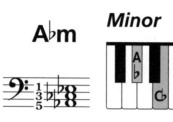

Diminished
A♭°

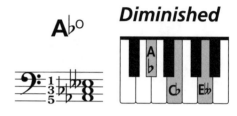

Augmented
A♭+

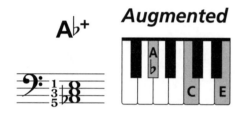

Major 7th
A♭maj⁷

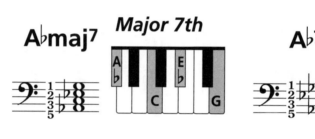

Dominant 7th
A♭7

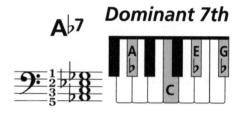

Minor 7th
A♭m⁷

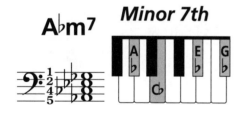

Diminished 7th
A♭°7

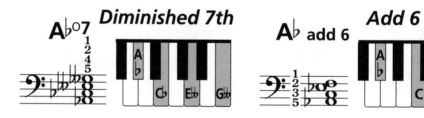

Add 6
A♭ add 6

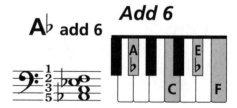

Inverting Chords

All of the chords on pages 94–110 are shown in *root position.* Any root position chord may be changed by moving the root (bottom note) of the chord to another position. This is called an *inversion*—it means the notes are rearranged and a note other than the root is the bottom note of the chord.

First Inversion

The first inversion of a C triad can be made by moving the root (C) to the top of the chord.

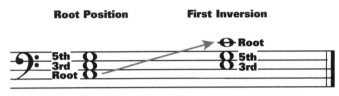

C E G   becomes   E G C

All letter names are the same, but the 3rd (E) is now on the bottom, and the root (C) is now on top. This is called *first inversion.*

Second Inversion

Any first inversion chord may be inverted again by moving the lowest note (3rd) to the top.

The second inversion can made from a first inversion C chord by moving the 3rd (E) to the top of the chord.

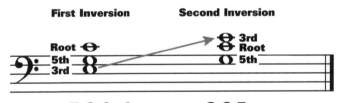

E G C   becomes   G C E

All letter names are the same, but the 5th (G) is now on the bottom, and the root (C) is now in the middle. This is called *second inversion.*

Inverting Four-Note Chords

Four-note chords such as 7th chords can also be inverted. Chords with four notes can be written in four different positions: root position, first inversion, second inversion and third inversion.

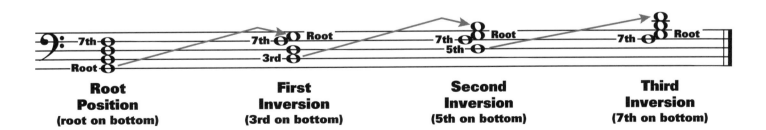

MAJOR SCALES

C Major Scale

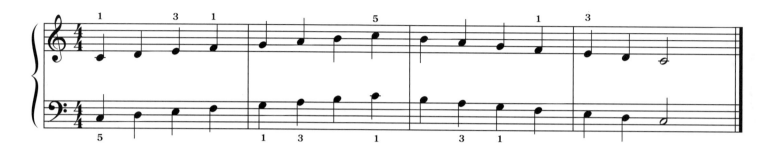

G Major Scale

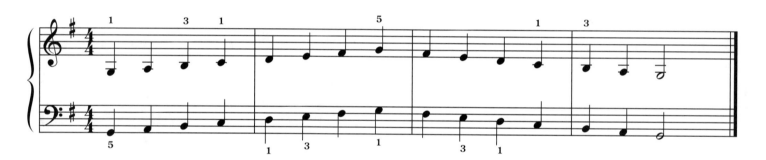

D Major Scale

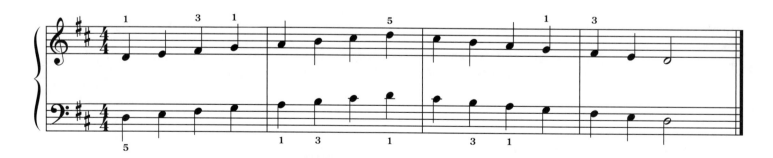

A Major Scale

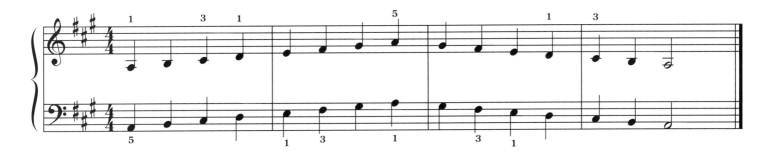

E Major Scale

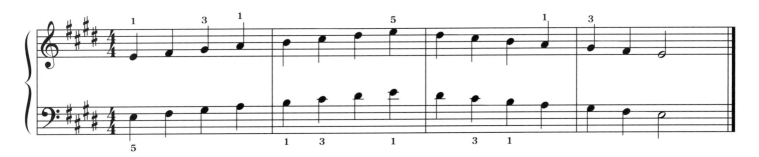

B Major Scale

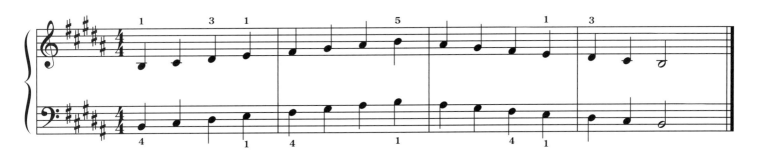

F♯ Major Scale

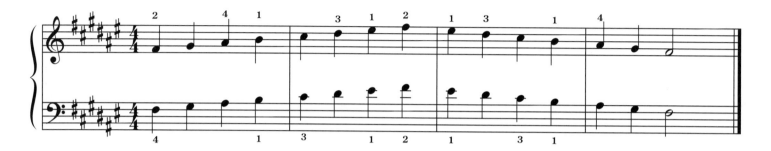

C♯ Major Scale

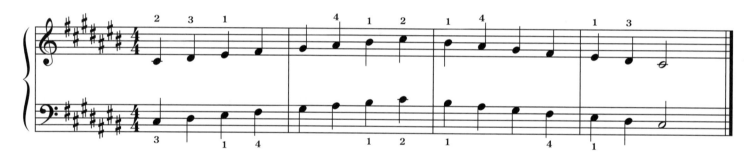

F Major Scale

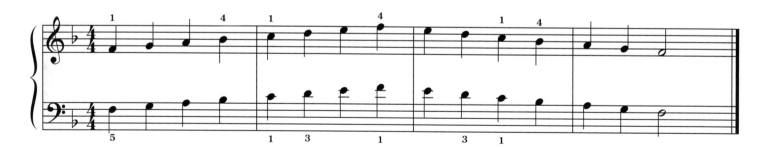

Bb Major Scale

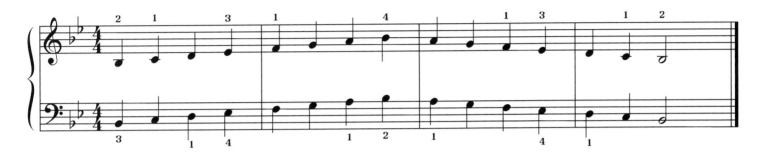

Eb Major Scale

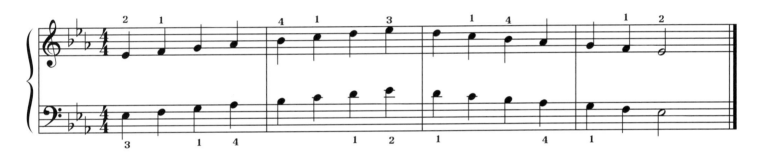

Ab Major Scale

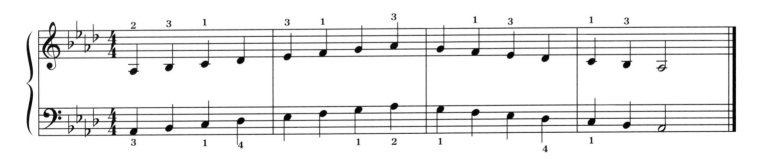

Db Major Scale

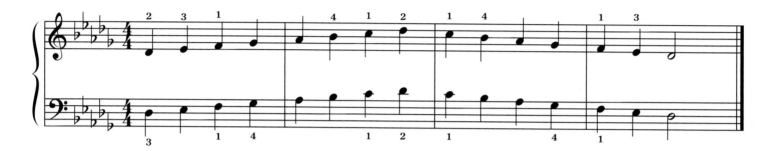

Gb Major Scale

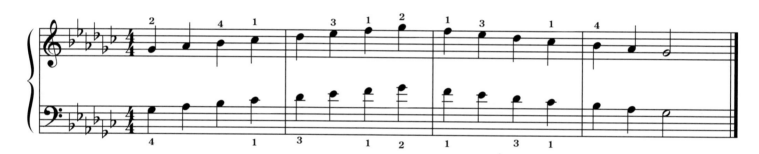

Cb Major Scale

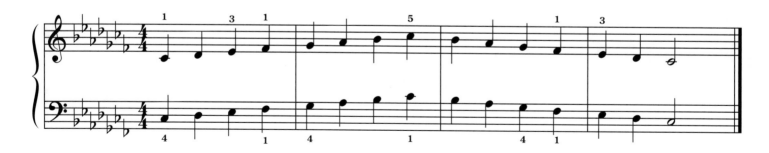

MINOR SCALES

A Natural Minor Scale

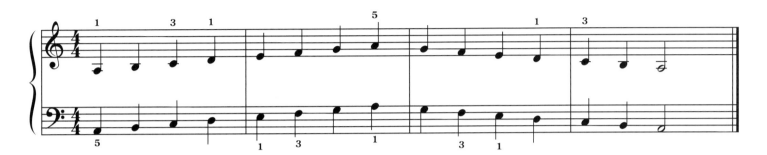

A Harmonic Minor Scale

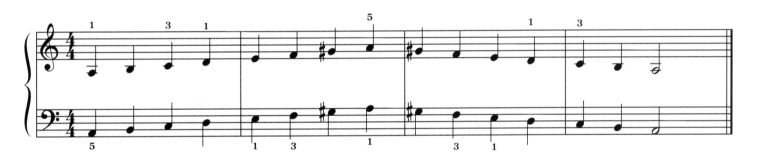

A Melodic Minor Scale

E Natural Minor Scale

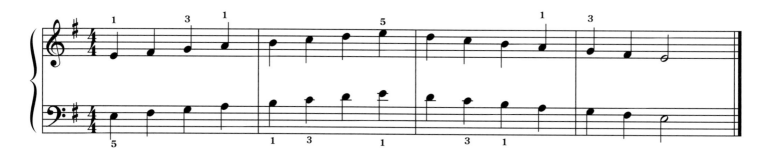

E Harmonic Minor Scale

E Melodic Minor Scale

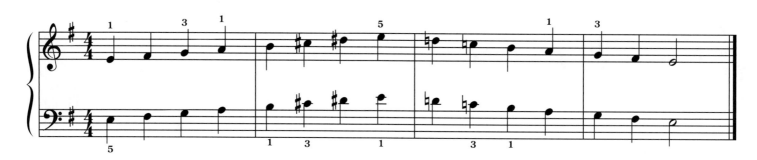

B Natural Minor Scale

B Harmonic Minor Scale

B Melodic Minor Scale

F# Natural Minor Scale

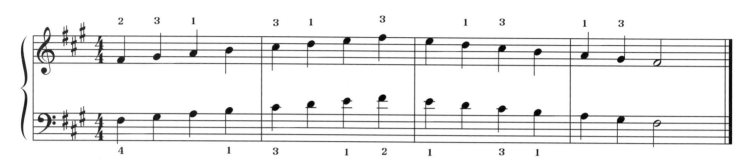

F# Harmonic Minor Scale

F# Melodic Minor Scale

C# Natural Minor Scale

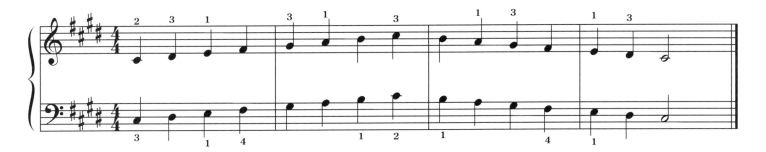

C# Harmonic Minor Scale

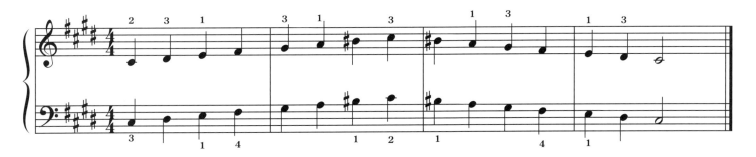

C# Melodic Minor Scale

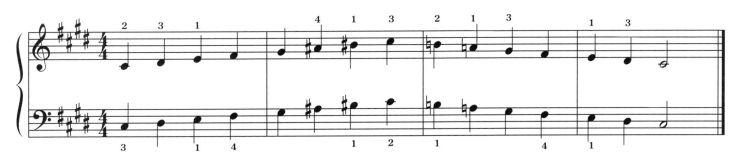

G♯ Natural Minor Scale

G♯ Harmonic Minor Scale

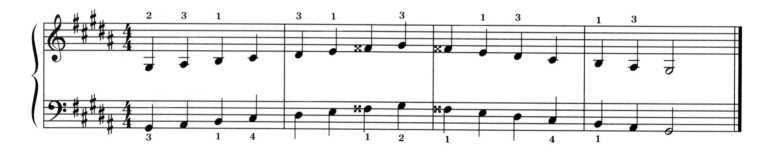

G♯ Melodic Minor Scale

D♯ Natural Minor Scale

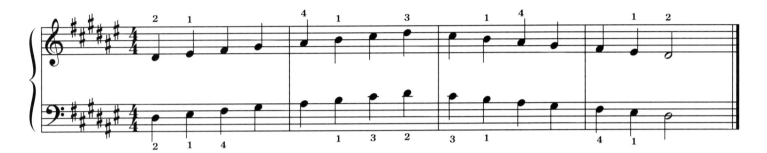

D♯ Harmonic Minor Scale

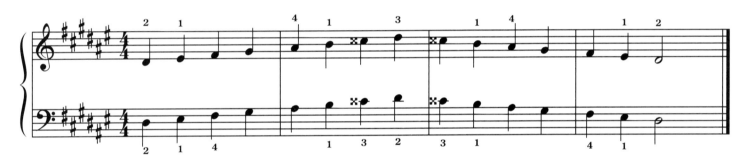

D♯ Melodic Minor Scale

A# Natural Minor Scale

A# Harmonic Minor Scale

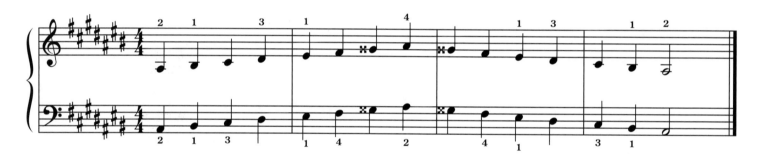

A# Melodic Minor Scale

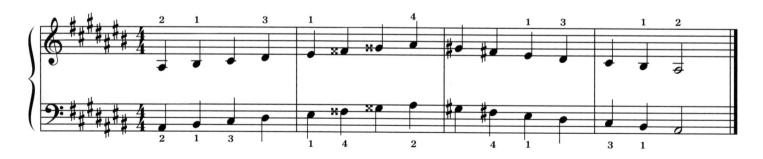

D Natural Minor Scale

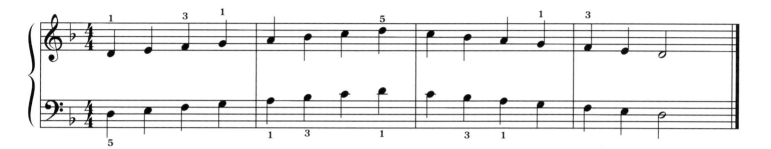

D Harmonic Minor Scale

D Melodic Minor Scale

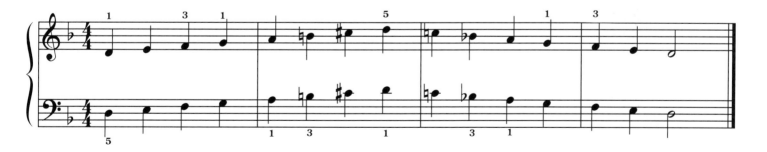

G Natural Minor Scale

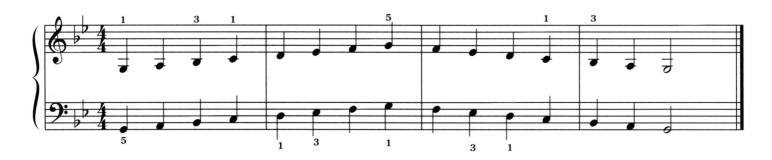

G Harmonic Minor Scale

G Melodic Minor Scale

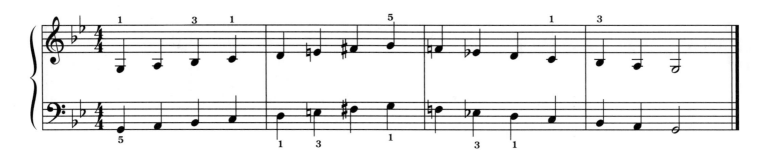

C Natural Minor Scale

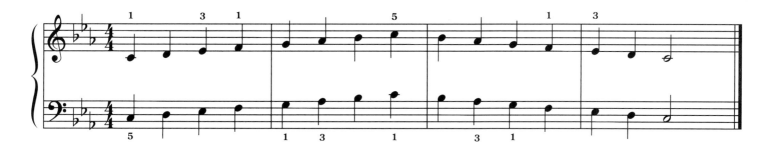

C Harmonic Minor Scale

C Melodic Minor Scale

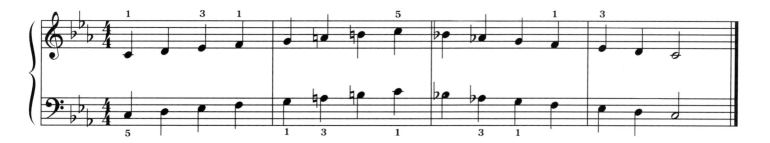

F Natural Minor Scale

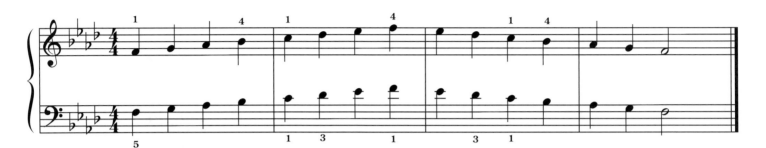

F Harmonic Minor Scale

F Melodic Minor Scale

B♭ Natural Minor Scale

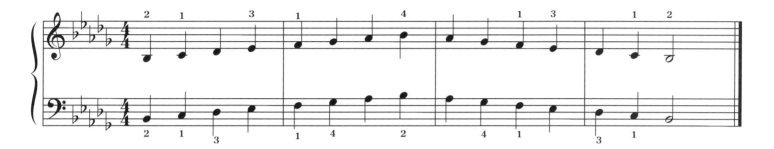

B♭ Harmonic Minor Scale

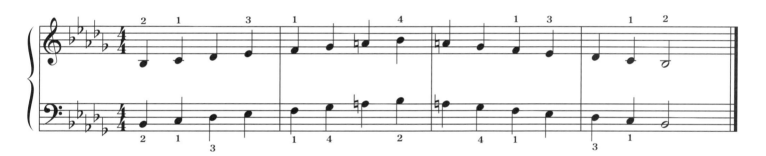

B♭ Melodic Minor Scale

E♭ Natural Minor Scale

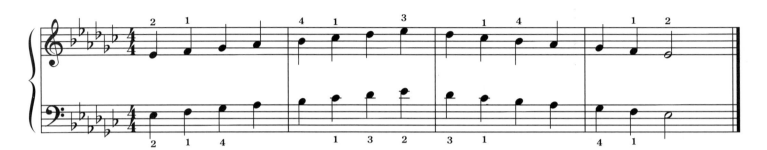

E♭ Harmonic Minor Scale

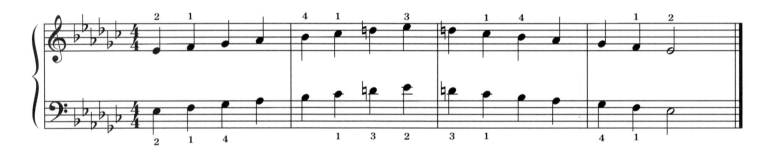

E♭ Melodic Minor Scale

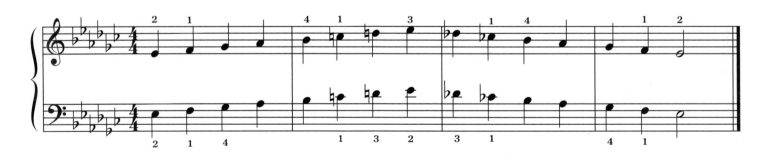

A♭ Natural Minor Scale

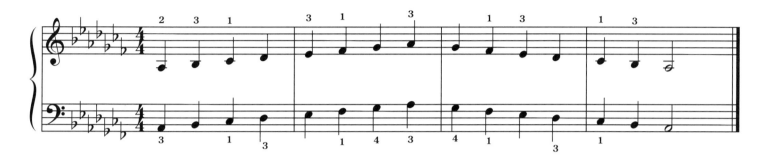

A♭ Harmonic Minor Scale

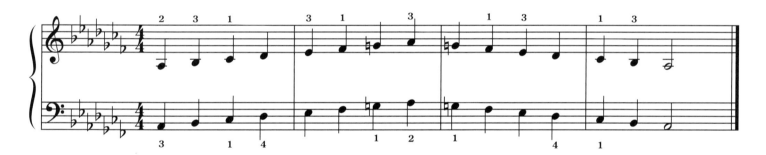

A♭ Melodic Minor Scale

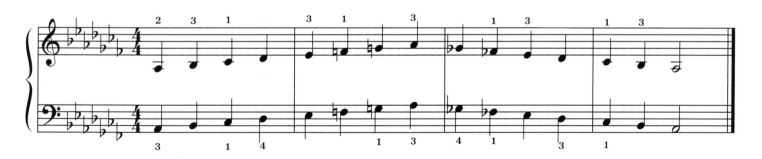

THE CIRCLE OF FIFTHS

The *circle of fifths* serves as a quick reference guide to the relationship of the keys and how key signatures can be figured out in a logical manner. Clockwise movement (up a 5th) provides all of the sharp keys by progressively adding one sharp to the key signature. Similarly, counter-clockwise (down a 5th) provides the flat keys by adding one flat.

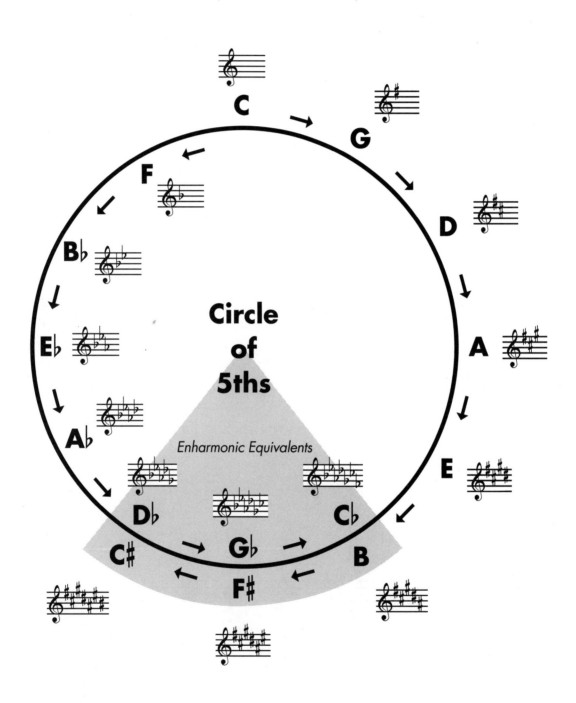